THE ECONOMICS OF
COLONIALISM IN
KOREA

THE ECONOMICS OF COLONIALISM IN
KOREA

Rethinking Japanese Rule and Aftermath

KIMURA Mitsuhiko

Publisher's Note

Japanese, Korean, and Chinese names are written family name first as is customary in East Asia. Charts in this book are excerpts of reference materials from more than fifty years ago and were arranged by the author. Please bear in mind that all possible measures were taken to receive permission from copyright holders to reproduce the charts appearing in this book. However, in some cases, information regarding the copyright was unknown. If you are the copyright holder for any of the charts in this book, please contact us.

The Economics of Colonialism in Korea: Rethinking Japanese Rule and Aftermath
Kimura Mitsuhiko. Translated by the Japan Institute of International Affairs (JIIA).

Published by
Japan Publishing Industry Foundation for Culture (JPIC)
2-2-30 Kanda-Jinbocho, Chiyoda-ku, Tokyo 101-0051, Japan

First English edition: March 2021

© 2018 Kimura Mitsuhiko
English translation © 2021 The Japan Institute of International Affairs (JIIA)
All rights reserved

Originally published in Japanese under the title of *Nihon tochika no Chosen: Tokei to jissho kenkyu wa nani o kataruka* by CHUOKORON-SHINSHA, INC., in 2018.
English publishing rights arranged with Kimura Mitsuhiko.

This publication is the result of a collaborative effort between the Japan Institute of International Affairs (JIIA) and Japan Publishing Industry Foundation for Culture (JPIC).

Jacket and cover illustration
Map (upper half): North Korean military parade marking the 70th anniversary of North Korea's founding (detail). Photo by Kyodo News.
(bottom half): Seoul cityscape (detail).

Book design: LampLighters Label

Printed in Japan
ISBN 978-4-86658-124-8
https://www.jpic.or.jp/

Dedication

In Bangkok in March 2017, Professor Hla Myint, my mentor at the London School of Economics and Political Science (LSE) in 1979–80, closed the final chapter for his 97-year life. He was a moderate libertarian and preached a development strategy that mixed appropriate government intervention and market economy. But in his homeland of Myanmar, the military regime advocated the "Burmese way to socialism" (Buddhist socialism) and maintained strict economic controls. As a result, the economy stagnated and the people were unable to free themselves from poverty. I clearly remember when Professor Myint declared despairingly to me, "What a silly government!" My communication with Professor Myint was cut off after he retired from LSE, but I was able to restore ties through Professor Emeritus Odaka Konosuke of Hitotsubashi University in 2015, a kindness for which I am very grateful. I think Professor Myint was blessed in his last years to see his homeland open up and democratize, albeit to a limited extent. Unfortunately, I did not get an opportunity to see him again, but his views remain much more than a passing thought to me, and I dedicate this book to him.

Preface to the English Edition

I wrote this book for the Japanese public at large (so there are no footnotes and very few references in the text). It was published in 2018 as *Nihon tochika no Chosen: Tokei to jissho kenkyu wa nani o kataruka* (Korea under Japanese Rule: What Do Statistics and Empirical Research Tell Us?). In the translation into English, I have made some minor revisions and changed the title to *The Economics of Colonialism in Korea: Rethinking Japanese Rule and Aftermath*. It would be my great pleasure as a Japanese researcher if this book is able to give foreign students new insights into the modern history of East Asia's economy.

What happened in Korea, from 1910 to 1945, when it was under Japanese rule? Many books have been written on this subject. Usually, they characterize the politics as oppressive, the economy as exploitative or larcenous, and the general result is one of impoverishment. In South Korea, of course, such judgments have been recognized as "correct" history, that is, the only legitimate version.

About twenty years ago, I was in Seoul and happened to see an educational television program aimed at high school students that was presented in the format of a practical class. The teacher was a prominent history professor who told the Korean students that the Japanese rule of Korea was the worst of all colonial regimes in the world. This was followed by a camera shot of the students nodding their heads in agreement.

Intellectuals in Japan more or less share this view of Japanese rule, and it has become commonly accepted by society at large. Any person expressing an opposing view—for example, that Japan also did positive things in Korea, like providing proper rule, and contributing to Korea's socio-economic development—is censured. No words are harsh enough for such apostasy, and anyone daring to do so is reviled for being unrepentant, reckless in language, reactionary, ultra-right wing, lacking in conscience, and uncomprehending of the suffering of others.

When I heard the Korean professor speak on television, I thought: "What is the basis for his assertion? Has he investigated all of the colonial regimes in the world and reached his conclusion through comparison? That would surely be impossible. What does 'worst' mean, anyway? One would have to explain the basis for calling something evil, provide a clear-cut definition, and measure its degree, yet this teacher said nothing about any of those things. Even if I understand the emotions behind his words, his conclusions can hardly be called scholarly." It is unlikely that the high school students listening to the lecture entertained any doubts, but I was left wondering just how solid an empirical foundation lay under South Korea's historical awareness of this period.

The usual image of Japan's Edo period used to be quite dark. For example, it was thought that under the feudalistic system, farmers suffered under harsh annual tax quotas; industrial technology was undeveloped, leaving handicrafts as the only alternative; and poverty produced a stagnant population. But if we adopt this view, the rapid modernization that occurred after the Meiji Restoration becomes difficult to explain. Isn't it possible that the Edo period also had some positive aspects? With this in mind, historians have proceeded to revise their views and emphasize developmental factors such as the increase in agricultural productivity, the growth of a market economy, improvements achieved in the lives of farmers, the intentional control of population, and the propagation of primary education.

What about Korea? Economic growth in postwar South Korea was certainly fast enough to stun the world, as referred to by the phrase "Miracle on the Han River." If the period of Japanese rule was so bleak, wouldn't that miracle have been impossible? Could South Korea have come so far if its starting point was zero or in negative territory? In contrast, what about North Korea? Currently, it is the only country in the growing region of East Asia that has been left behind. Its economy is weak, making it one of the most impoverished nations in the world. What connection, if any, does that condition have to do with the period of Japanese rule? Was Japanese rule really that dark? There is only one way to answer these questions: through steady and thorough empirical research.

In 1971, Yamabe Kentaro published the monograph *Nihon tochika no Chosen* (Korea under Japanese Rule) as part of the Iwanami Shinsho series. He discusses Korea from both political and economic perspectives. Hailed as a great book, it has continued to be read to the present day (although it is now out of print). Yamabe was a communist and spent the war years in prison. After the war, he worked for the headquarters of the Japanese Communist Party and later began authoring books about Korea. As this background might suggest, the above-mentioned monograph vehemently condemns Japanese rule of Korea. Of course, certain elements of his criticism rightfully elicit agreement, including the various policies that robbed the Korean people of their ethnic dignity, as well as the all-out war policies adopted in the 1940s. However, the book's foregone conclusions are strongly colored by Yamabe's ideology, and the content clearly lacks balance.

In this book, I wish to present a thoroughly empirical discussion of Korea under Japanese rule that eschews ideology and adopts an economic focus. Fortunately, research in this field has made excellent progress in recent years, with arguments now emerging that completely change formerly accepted viewpoints. Much of this progress is due to advances in the collection and analysis of statistical data. In the following pages, I incorporate the results of this latest research while pursuing my argument.

Generally speaking, this book paints a very different picture of Korea under Japanese rule than that presented by Yamabe. It also clarifies some significant facts that have been buried for many years (for example, the fact that the roots of North Korea's nuclear development lie in the period of Japanese rule).

I can experience no greater joy than if this work contributes in some small way to a deeper general understanding of Japanese rule of Korea, and by extension, helps to promote true friendship and amity between Japan and South Korea.

Kimura Mitsuhiko
February 1, 2021
Aoyama, Tokyo

Acknowledgements

In my studies to date, I have benefited greatly from the assistance and input of many specialists. For issues in modern Korean history, I received entry-level instruction from Professor Emeritus An Byeong-jik at Seoul National University. Many others also helped me, and I deeply appreciate each person who taught me.

Professor Emeritus Inoki Takenori at Osaka University advised me to write this book. In addition to learning much from him and enjoying his friendship, I am greatly indebted to him for introducing me to publishers for the books I have written, including this one. He also provided in-depth comments on this volume, for which I thank him deeply. Hatayama Yasuyuki, head of the Contemporary Culture Research Center for East Asia, introduced me to the book by Han Yeong-u discussed in column 5 in chapter 6. Kimizuka Seika and Chiba Mitsuhiko helped organize, edit, and proofread my manuscript. At the time, they were respectively undergraduate and postgraduate students at Aoyama Gakuin University. Associate Professor Matsutani Motokazu of Tohoku Gakuin University pointed out several issues with the manuscript. My long-time collaborator Abe Keiji shared his ideas and literary knowledge with an openness that is usual for him, but unusual among university researchers. Shirato Naoto of Chuokoron-Shinsha demonstrated his mastery in producing pocket-size books while mitigating my written Japanese shortcomings. If the book is even a little easier to read, I owe that to Mr. Shirato. Finally, I would like to mention the cooperation and encouragement of my wife, Yoko, who also is very good with words. I thank everyone involved from the bottom of my heart.

I am also very grateful for the full support of the Japan Institute of International Affairs and the Japan Publishing Industry Foundation for Culture, and further, to an anonymous translator who worked hard to produce the English edition of this book. I take responsibility for any errors remaining in the text.

TABLE OF CONTENTS

INTRODUCTION

Initial Conditions
17

CHAPTER

3

Standards of Living
99

CHAPTER

4

Rapid Transition to the Wartime Economy:
From the Sino-Japanese War until the Fall of the Empire
117

CHAPTER

5

Emergence of North and South Korea:
The Legacy of the Japanese Empire
175

CHAPTER

6

What Did Japan Gain from Its Rule over Korea?
193

Korean Peninsula during Japanese Rule

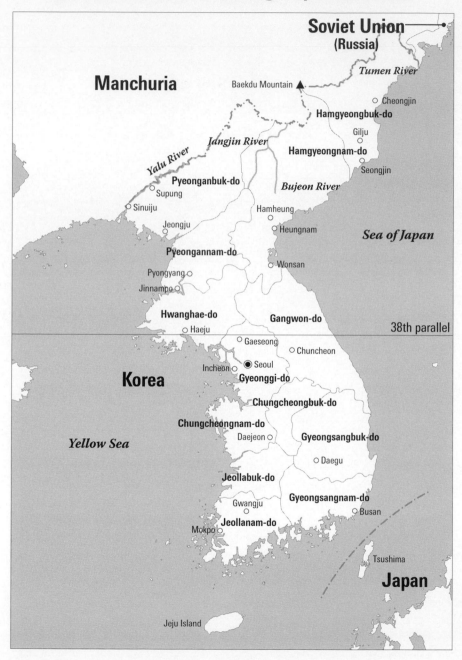

Korean History Prior to Annexation
(See the Chronology at end of this book)

After Japan won the Sino-Japanese War (1894–1895), the Korean dynasty was released from its allegiance as a vassal state to the Qing dynasty. In 1897, to proclaim both domestically and abroad that Korea had become a completely independent nation, King Gojong assumed the title of Emperor, thereby placing himself on the same level as the Emperor of the Qing dynasty, and changed the name of the state from the "Joseon dynasty" to the "Korean Empire."

The Russo-Japanese War began in February 1904 and lasted 19 months (ending with the signing of the Treaty of Portsmouth in September 1905). During that time, the First Japan-Korea Convention was signed in August 1904, on the basis of which the Japanese government installed either Japanese or other non-Korean advisers in such crucial Korean governmental departments as finance, foreign affairs, education, and police.

In November 1905, Japan gained authority over the foreign affairs of the Korean Empire through the signing of the Second Japan-Korea Convention. In 1906, the Japanese government established the Residency -General of Korea in the capital city of the Korean Empire, Hanseong (Kanjo, present-day Seoul), with Ito Hirobumi serving as the first resident-general. Later, on the basis of the Third Japan-Korea Convention, the Residency-General of Korea obtained expanded authority not only in foreign affairs but also Korea's internal governance.

In August 1910, Japan annexed the Korean Empire and designated it as a region called Joseon (Chosen) within the Japanese Empire. The Residency-General of Korea was replaced by the Government-General of Korea, with Army General Terauchi Masatake serving as the first governor-general. Hanseong was renamed Gyeongseong (Keijo).

Note to the Reader

Bearing in mind the partition of Korea after Japan's defeat in World War II, the area of the Korean Peninsula roughly north of the 38th parallel during the period of Japanese rule is referred to as "northern Korea" and the area south of that line as "southern Korea." In some cases, it is merely "North" and "South."

During the period of Japanese rule of Korea, Japan and the Japanese were referred to in Japanese as *naichi* (mainland) and *naichi-jin* (mainlanders), respectively, as distinct from Korea and the Koreans. But many postwar publications simply refer to the mainland during that period as *Nihon* or *Nippon* (Japan). In the original Japanese edition of this book, out of respect for historical terminology, when indicating the region or its people during the period of Japanese rule in Korea, Japan and the Japanese are referred to as *naichi* and *naichi-jin*.

In the English edition, the names of Korean places have been romanized according to the system revised in 2000 by the National Academy of the Korean Language, Ministry of Culture and Tourism of the Republic of Korea, with some exceptions such as Pyongyang (Pyeongyang). The capital city of the Korean dynasty was commonly called Seoul and this continued, among Koreans, into the early years of Japanese rule, so Seoul has been used in the English edition of this book.

INTRODUCTION

Initial Conditions

What were the economic conditions like in Korea in the early 1910s, just after annexation? I begin by exploring this question, including the effects that natural conditions had on the economy.

1. Natural Conditions on the Korean Peninsula

Continental Topography and Climate

Korea's northern border with Manchuria (now northeastern China) is defined by the Tumen River to the east and the Yalu River to the west. Both rivers are larger than any rivers in Japan in terms of both volume of flow and length: the Tumen River is 521 kilometers long and the Yalu River is 791 kilometers, whereas the Shinano River, the longest river in Japan, is 367 kilometers. The Yalu River in particular, as well as tributaries such as the Bujeon and Jangjin rivers, had great potential for hydroelectric power generation.

Most of the eastern part of northern Korea consists of mountains and highlands. In the western part, mountains extend northward. From Pyongyang and its outskirts, plains extend to the coastal areas on the Yellow Sea. In southern Korea, the land tends to be mountainous in the eastern and central areas, but plains are relatively numerous in the southwest.

Compared with Japan, the climate in Korea is continental, meaning that it is dry with little rain and has cold winters and hot summers. Because spring comes late and autumn comes early, northern Korea is ill-suited to double cropping. However, temperatures in August exceed 20 degrees Celsius on average and can climb to almost 30 degrees. Therefore, with the exception of certain areas, rice cultivation is possible. In southern Korea, double cropping is done primarily in the southern area.

Untapped Mineral Resources

Gold and silver have been mined since ancient times on the Korean Peninsula, especially in the north. For example, the Geomdeok mine in the northeastern part of northern Korea has been known as a large silver mine since the middle ages. That mine has a connection with Japan, as well. When Toyotomi Hideyoshi invaded Korea in the sixteenth century, the mine was placed under the control of Kato Kiyomasa (a well-known samurai who served under Hideyoshi). Located in the western part of northern Korea, the Unsan gold mine was another famous mine.

The Korean dynasty did not actively develop gold and silver mines, however, for various reasons: they feared an outflow of gold and silver to the Ming and Qing dynasties in China, placed a strong ideological emphasis on agriculture, and lacked well-developed mining technologies. In Japan, gold and silver production increased dramatically from the Sengoku period (the sixteenth century), providing the foundation for the development of a money economy during the Edo period (1603–1867). Although this difference between the two countries is well worth further study from the perspective of comparative history, it falls outside the scope of this book.

Fields of anthracite existed in Pyongyang. During the Korean dynasty period, villagers living near Pyongyang used anthracite in small amounts for heating and cooking. It was the Imperial Japanese Navy that first showed strong interest in the Pyongyang Coal Field because anthracite burns without smoke, making it difficult to detect and thus perfect for use by warships. The Japanese Navy began surveying the anthracite fields in Pyongyang as early as the 1880s (at the time, Japan was producing more than 1 million tons of coal annually, but most of it was bituminous coal, and only a small proportion of the total output was anthracite). There were also several iron mines in the Pyongyang area.

Northern Korea had a variety of other mineral resources that could not be found in Japan. The history of geologic formation on the Korean Peninsula (especially in the north) was similar to that of Manchuria and northern China and very different from that of the Japanese archipelago. Most of these underground resources were left unexplored and untouched until Japanese rule, particularly after 1930, when they were discovered. I discuss this point in more detail later.

2. A Society Dependent on Traditional Agriculture

Low Agricultural Productivity

Recent research shows that Korea had a total population of 15 to 16 million people at the time of annexation (about one-third of the 50 million people living in Japan at the same time). According to statistics compiled by the Government-General of Korea, about 80 percent of all households in Korea in 1910 were farming households (table 0-1). In contrast, households engaged in commerce and industry were quite rare. In the early 1870s in Japan, about 70 percent of the working population were engaged in agriculture and forestry. This indicates that, at the time of annexation, the Korean economy was more dependent on agriculture than the Japanese economy had been at the beginning of the Meiji era (1868–1912), some 40 years earlier.

Most agriculture in northern Korea centered on a single dry-field crop every year, with a secondary emphasis on three crops grown every two years. Slash-and-burn (known as *hwajeon* in Korean) techniques were common, and there was much fallow land. In contrast, double

Table 0-1.

Breakdown of Korean Household Occupations as of December 31, 1910

(1,000 households)

Farming	2,337	*Yangban* (ruling class)	61
Fishing	36	*Yusaeng* (Confucian scholar)	21
Manufacturing	29	Day worker	94
Mining	4	Other	41
Commerce	185	Unemployed	31
Government employee	16	Total	2,855

Note: This survey was conducted among heads of households; those pursuing two or three different occupations concurrently were counted in each category, and therefore, the total does not match the actual number of households. Those in the *yangban* category are the descendants of civil servants and military officers; those in the *yusaeng* category make their household living through the study of Chinese classics.
Source: The Government-General of Korea 1912, *Chosen Sotokufu tokei nempo: Meiji 43 nen*, 125–126.

cropping was the norm in southern Korea, and paddy agriculture throve in the southernmost region, often with rice planted first and wheat, barley, or another crop planted later.

In the north, the greatest amount of cultivated land was dedicated to millet. In the eastern part of northern Korea, millet was followed by barley, Japanese millet, and soybeans. In the western part, millet was followed by rice and soybeans. Maize, which became the dietary mainstay of North Korea after the war, was not grown much outside of Pyeongan-buk-do in the northwest.

Rice was the most common crop in southern Korea, followed by barley and soybeans. Annual rice yield in the north was about 0.8 *koku* (brown rice, about 120 kilograms) per *tan* (about 10 ares, 1 are = 100 m²); in the south, it was about 1.0 *koku* per *tan*. The average rice yield in Japan as a whole exceeded 1.0 *koku* per *tan* in the 1880s and climbed to nearly 2.0 *koku* per *tan* in the first decade of the twentieth century. Around 1910, 1.5 *koku* per *tan* was standard in northeastern Japan. Compared with these figures, the productivity of land used to cultivate rice in Korea was very low. According to recent research, the amount of rice produced throughout Korea on a per capita basis averaged 0.67 *koku* between 1911 and 1913. This, too, was lower than the average per capita amount produced in Japan during the early Meiji period, which was 0.73 *koku* from 1874 to 1876.

Low productivity in rice cultivation was due in large part to technical problems. There were few irrigation systems in place in Korea, so that the majority of rice fields depended either wholly or in great part on natural irrigation (i.e., the fields had an unstable water supply). Most farming families supplied their own fertilizer, which consisted of such materials as manure ash, animal manure, and green manure. Manure ash was made by combining the ash residue from fuel burned in Korean floor heaters (*ondol*) with human waste. It was also common for farmers to cultivate dry fields without using fertilizer at all. At the time of annexation, dried sardines and animal bones (cattle, pigs, dogs) were produced in large quantities, but they were mostly exported to Japan and not used domestically as fertilizer.

Korean farmers used cultivating techniques for dry field farming that differed from those used in Japan. Generally, these were considered old-fashioned under Japanese rule. After World War II, however, they were reevaluated as techniques that, while crude, were well adapted to natural conditions. For example, the combination of millet and soybeans or adzuki beans, either through mixed cultivation or intercropping, was a rational approach that helped avoid total loss under conditions that tended to be dry with irregular rainfall. Crop rotation of three crops every two years, particularly as practiced in the western part of northern Korea, has now come to be viewed as an excellent cultivation method. Through the alternating cultivation of gramineous species such as wheat, barley, and millet with leguminous species such as soybeans and adzuki beans, the fertility of the soil could be maintained even with low levels of fertilization.

One non-food crop that deserves special mention is cotton. It was grown in many locations in the southernmost part of southern Korea but was limited to the southwestern region in northern Korea. The cotton was used as raw material for making traditional cloth that was hand-woven by the farmers.

The Importance of Cattle for Field Cultivation, Food, and Transport

In the early 1910s, Japan and Korea were each home to about 1.3 million head of domesticated cattle. The comparative per-capita abundance of cattle in Korea is noteworthy, being particularly numerous in the eastern part of northern Korea (Hamgyeongbuk-do and Hamgyeongnam-do) in relation to the number of farming families.

Korean cattle (yellow cattle) were far superior to Japanese cattle in terms of physical build, fertility, stamina, and ability to withstand a poor diet and unfavorable environmental conditions. They also had calm and wise dispositions that, according to some observers, made them surprisingly docile when following the commands of their masters. Korean farmers had traditionally cared for their cattle as if they were part of the family and worked hard to breed and improve them. Those efforts were rewarded in the superior characteristics of their cattle. Korean farmers used cattle between the ages of about three to eight years old to work the fields and pull loads, after which they sold the cattle for meat.

For field cultivation, Koreans did not customarily use horses, which were few in number and had weak constitutions. Even in small fields, farmers used cattle instead of human labor to till the soil. Traditionally, they calculated land area in terms of how many days it took to cultivate it with cattle, revealing the universality and importance of cattle-based cultivation. In general, farmers in the north plowed with two oxen, while those in the south used only a single ox. They were highly skilled at handling their cattle and even children were adept at doing so.

Japanese observers at the time of annexation pointed out various factors that contributed to the development of cattle husbandry and cattle-based cultivation in Korea, including the relative sparseness of the human population compared with the land area, the presence of ample fields and mountains where cattle could pasture, the suitability of natural features and climate, and Korean proficiency in raising and managing cattle. These are, however, nothing more than superficial observations. Within the overall context of East and Southeast Asia, the conditions cited for Korea are not unusual. On the contrary, it is early-modern Japan that can be considered atypical in this regard. As is well known, the use of cattle (and horses) declined in Japan and cultivation came to be carried out primarily through human labor. In Japanese economic history, this phenomenon is often referred to as the "Industrious Revolution." It was not, however, a universal phenomenon throughout Korea and the rest of Asia. The surprise evidenced by the Japanese observers concerning Korean agricultural practice was a result of their inability to escape the narrow perspective of their native country.

Cattle were useful for more than field cultivation and food. Oxcarts provided a common means of transportation in Korea. Contracted transportation services were an important side business for farming families, especially in the northeastern part of northern Korea, where it was impossible to grow crops during the winter. Manure and bones provided raw materials for fertilizer, and cowhide was used for the manufacture of army boots, horse tack, and other products. Even before annexation, Korea exported large amounts of live cattle, leather, and cattle bones to Japan and the Russian Far East.

There is a proverb from a region in the eastern part of northern Korea that goes, "A family won't be impoverished by the loss of an elderly father, but it will by the loss of a cow." This hints at how important cattle were to Korean farmers.

Periodic Markets Distributed Evenly throughout Korea

Urban commerce lagged behind that of Japan, as evidenced by the size of cities. In 1910, Seoul, the largest city in Korea, had a population of just 278,000 people (of whom about 38,000 were Japanese). No other city in Korea had a population of more than 100,000. The total population of Busan, the second-largest city, was 71,000. Pyongyang, the largest city in northern Korea, had fewer than 40,000 inhabitants.

For farmers, the usual venues for commercial transactions were periodic markets held every five days, where they bought and sold food, daily produce, or local specialized goods by either using copper coins or bartering. One characteristic of these markets was their even geographical distribution, which put a market within a day's walk of nearly every farmer in Korea (because the south was relatively densely populated, there were more markets there than in the north). In each region, markets located close to each other were held on different days so that, in principle, a farmer could go to market on any day and conduct transactions. Over the course of time, a market network developed throughout Korea and achieved geographic equilibrium (Kimura 1986).

There were various kinds of specialized tradesmen, including itinerant vendors who made the rounds of the periodic markets, urban vendors who operated stores in urban centers, and wholesalers who engaged in long-distance trade. During the Korean dynasty period, the tradesmen based in Seoul and Gaeseong were especially well known. The former monopolized the supply of necessities to the royal court, and the latter had control of ginseng distribution.

Underdeveloped Industry

At the time of annexation, there were very few modern factories in Korea. In 1911, 252 factories throughout Korea were equipped with motors, and 75 of these were dedicated to modest rice-polishing operations. The total horsepower of the motors in operation in these factories was only slightly more than 6,000 hp. Sixty percent of that was concentrated in the nine plants operating in the gas and electric power sectors, and 90 percent or more of the capital in these factories was Japanese.

Most of the industry pursued by Koreans themselves was composed of side businesses operated manually by farmers. There were a few specialized enterprises that employed workers, but their numbers were small. Principal products included miso, soy sauce, sake, and other processed foods, as well as textiles. Processed foods were produced by farming families mainly for their own consumption.

The rural cotton industry, particularly cotton yarn production, declined after Korean ports were opened to trade in 1876, which led to the importation of manufactured goods from Japan and Great Britain. Even so, 250,000 households were engaged in the production of cotton yarn and 480,000 in the production of cotton cloth throughout Korea in 1911. It was usual for each household to have a hand-made wooden loom to produce white cotton cloth for family use (Kimura 2016, 12).

Hemp fabric was needed by Koreans for summer clothing and for use in funeral rites. In 1911, it was produced by 360,000 farming households. Production was centered in Gyeongsangbuk-do and Gyeongsangnam-do in the southeastern part of southern Korea and in Hamgyeongnam-do in the eastern part of northern Korea.

Sericulture, silk-thread spinning, and silk weaving were practiced throughout Korea. Yeongheung-gun in Hamgyeongnam-do in northern Korea was famous as a region for sericulture. Farming families that raised silkworms in this region did not weave silk themselves; instead, they sold the cocoons through brokers. Farming families that bought the cocoons spun thread from them by hand, without the use of machinery. The main silk product produced was pongee, which was sold to the upper-class. In the western part of northern Korea, the counties of Deokcheon, Taecheon, Yeongbyeon, Uiju, and Guseong were known as pongee production centers; Taecheon and Yeongbyeon were particularly well known. In southern Korea, Gyeongsangbuk-do, particularly Sangju, was the main production center of pongee.

3. Food Consumption and Education Level

A Main Diet of Minor Grains with Wild Plants and Grasses as Important Supplements

In Japan in the second half of the nineteenth century, many rural households could not afford to eat rice on a daily basis. This was especially true in northeastern Japan and in communities located in mountainous areas. In Korea, which was less productive than Japan, even fewer households could eat rice on a regular basis. Those who could were limited to wealthy families in cities and upper-class farmers. For the general population, the basic meal was made up of minor grains, even in rice-producing areas.

In rice-producing areas in the western part of northern Korea, for example, farmers belonging to the middle class or lower almost never ate rice. Their usual diet consisted of grains such as millet, adzuki beans, Japanese millet, and barley. These were supplemented by vegetables pickled in salt, with many households also harvesting wild plants in the spring and early summer. Other supplemental foods included dried fish, beef, pork, chicken, and dog meat, although opportunities to eat these were few. According to a survey conducted in 1915 in Hamgyeongbuk-do in the northeastern part of northern Korea, fewer than one percent of the population ate rice on a regular basis, and most of them lived in cities (Cheongjin and Seongjin). More than half of the regional population did not eat rice even once over the period of a year (*Chosen nokaiho* 1916, 11 (6), 67–68).

The same was true in the south. According to a survey conducted in rice-producing Jeollabuk-do in 1913, 11,000 "upper-class" households, or just 6 percent of the 191,000 total farming households in the surveyed area, were able to eat rice year-round. About 41,000 middle-class households (22%) could eat rice for about six months of the year starting with the fall rice harvest; they switched to wheat and barley for six months after the barley harvest in May. About 79,000 lower-class households (42%) ate a mix of rice, barley, millet, and vegetables after the rice harvest and switched to barley after the barley harvest. There were also 58,000 subsistence farming households (31%) who could not eat three meals a day year-round and had trouble managing two or even one meal a day (Kishi 1914, 13–14). Under these circumstances, famine often arose in both the north and the south during the Korean dynasty period. In 1909, just before annexation, a famine occurred in Muncheon-gun in Hamgyeongnam-do in northern Korea, with many farmers eating bean gruel, grass roots, and tree bark to stay alive. Many crossed the border to live in Manchuria.

Plants that grew naturally in mountains and fields were a precious food source for Korean farmers. Typical examples included wild rocambole, bracken fern, dandelion, Japanese parsley, Chinese bellflower, creeper, chickweed, shepherd's purse, and Japanese bindweed. In addition, there was widespread use of cooking methods for the preparation of emergency foods, such as pulverizing kudzu root, the inner bark of pine, or millet stalk and using the resulting powder to make gruel or dumplings.

Education Level: Confucianism and the Primacy of Males
A traditional system of primary education called *seodang* existed in Korea before annexation by Japan. It is said that the origins of this system reach all the way back to the medieval Goryeo period. The *seodang*

system, which resembled the *terakoya* schools of Japan, consisted of private schools in which one teacher instructed about 10 students. However, there were two rather pronounced differences. First, unlike *terakoya* schools in Japan, which had a fair number of female students, *seodang* schools were attended almost exclusively by male students. Second, *terakoya* schools included commercial skills, farming, and other practical content in their curricula, whereas *seodang* schools were almost completely dedicated to Confucian classics.

With the advent of the Korean Empire, there was a great flowering of modern private schools founded by intellectuals. Most of these were small-scale institutions offering primary or secondary education. During the period when Korea was ruled by the Residency-General of Korea, schools comparable to regular primary schools in Japan (*futsu gakko*) were opened for Korean students in the cities such as Seoul and Busan. These schools continued to be administered by the Government-General after annexation.

According to statistics compiled by the Government-General, there were 16,540 *seodang* schools all over Korea in 1912, far outnumbering the modern private and official schools combined. However, because their average size was so small, they only served a total of about 140,000 students (Kimura 2016, 20).

In 1912, the ratio of children attending school in Korea, including those attending *seodang* schools, to the overall population was 1.4 percent. If we refer to data from later years and assume that the school-age demographic was between 15 percent and 20 percent of the total population, we arrive at an overall enrollment rate of 7 percent to 9 percent. In 1873, 40 percent of all primary-school aged boys and 15 percent of all primary-school aged girls were attending school in Japan. Compared with these numbers, the enrollment rate in Korea at the time of annexation was very low. The dissemination rate of primary education in Japan in the early Meiji era was based on accomplishments in the Edo period. Primary education was therefore less developed in Korea than in Japan before the modern period.

Because education in *seodang* schools was limited almost exclusively to boys, girls had virtually no educational opportunities. According to a national census conducted in 1930, more than 90 percent of women 40 years old and over reported that they could not read or write Hangul. These statistics give us insight into the lack of female education under dynastic rule.

The *seodang* educational system was more broadly disseminated in the north than in the south. Traditionally, Confucianism flourished more in the south, particularly in Gyeongsang-do. The south also had more Confucian scholars (see the note to table 0-1). In light of this, it would be natural to assume that the dissemination rate of primary education would be relatively higher in the south as well, but the opposite was true. The reason for this is unclear. One possible explanation is that the *yangban* (ruling class) who carried on the Confucian tradition repressed the education of commoners. Knowledge of Confucianism was a prerequisite for high social standing in Korea, and the ruling class may have seen an advantage in monopolizing educational opportunity. Because the power of the *yangban* was weaker in the north, they may have been less able to repress education among commoners.

CHAPTER
1

Japanese Administrative Policies in Korea
A Public Finance Perspective

The characteristics of a government are most clearly expressed by the way it constructs public finance. This can be considered a general axiom regardless of the time, country, or region in question. Therefore, chapter 1 is dedicated to a detailed examination of the public finance of the Residency-General and the Government-General of Korea until 1936. Public finance after 1936 will be discussed in chapter 4.

Before getting into the main issue, let us review a related topic, that is, changes in governmental organization and workforce.

1. Organization and Workforce of the Government-General of Korea

An Expanding Government

Tables 1-1, 1-2, and 1-3 present organizational charts of the Government-General of Korea in 1912, 1922, and 1935, respectively. In the early years, the chart reflects an organization inherited from the Residency-General of Korea (table 1-1). After the Banzai Sojo Incident (the anti-Japanese independence movement of March 1, 1919), the Government-General undertook major organizational reforms, and table 1-2 shows the results of those reforms and how the government was organized in 1922. Table 1-3 shows the organizational structure as it stood thirteen years later in 1935.

Even a cursory glance reveals that the government expanded during this period. The number of departments and bureaus in the central government (including the Secretariat) increased from five to seven and ultimately to eight, with even greater increases in the number of affiliated offices, rising from 20 to 22 and then to 32. This kind of expansion may seem natural and not worth special mention, but the conspicuous changes that occurred in just over twenty years have deep significance. They show that the Government-General greatly increased its activity in various administrative areas, meaning that it played an expanded governmental role.

Table 1-1.

Organizational Chart of the Government-General of Korea as of April 1912

The Government-General of Korea
- Secretariat
- Home Affairs Department
- Finance Department
- Agriculture, Commerce and Industry Department
- Justice Department

Affiliated Offices
- Central Council
- Provincial Governments
- Police Affairs Department
- Law Court
- Prisons
- Railway Bureau
- Communications Bureau
- Bureau of Provisional Cadastral Survey
- Custom House
- Forestry Station
- The Government-General Hospital
- Social Welfare Institution
- Pyongyang Mining Office
- Model Farm
- Central Laboratory
- Civil Engineering Committee
- Korea Taxation Petition Investigation Committee
- Higher Cadastral Survey Committee
- Regional Cadastral Survey Committee
- Schools

Note: Tables 1-1 to 1-3 reflect the original materials, except for some portions that were revised to omit smaller bureaucratic divisions and offices.
Sources: The Government-General of Korea 1922, 36–37, inserted figure; The Government-General of Korea 1999, (2), 1–4, appended table; and Hagiwara 2001a, 54–56.

Table 1-2.

Organizational Chart of the Government-General of Korea as of March 31, 1922

The Government-General of Korea
- Secretariat
- Home Affairs Bureau
- Financial Bureau
- Industrial Bureau
- Judicial Bureau
- Education Bureau
- Police Bureau

Affiliated Offices
- Central Council
- Provincial Governments
- Police Training Institute
- Communications Bureau
- Maritime Tribunal
- Monopoly Bureau
- Custom House
- Law Court
- Prisons
- Forestry Station
- The Government-General Hospital
- Social Welfare Institution
- Pyongyang Mining Office
- Model Farm
- Central Laboratory
- Bovine Infectious Disease Serum Factory
- Fishery Experimental Station
- Civil Engineering Committee
- Korea Taxation Petition Investigation Committee
- Higher Cadastral Survey Committee
- Forest Cadastral Survey Committee
- Government Schools

Table 1-3.

Organizational Chart of the Government-General of Korea as of August 31, 1935

The Government-General of Korea
- Secretariat
- Home Affairs Bureau
- Financial Bureau
- Industrial Bureau
- Agriculture and Forestry Bureau
- Judicial Bureau
- Educational Bureau
- Police Bureau

Affiliated Offices
- Central Council
- Communications Bureau
- Railway Bureau
- Monopoly Bureau
- Provincial Governments
- Taxation Supervision Office
- Custom House
- Law Court
- Prisons
- Police Training School
- Public Depositories
- Forestry Station
- Social Welfare Institution
- Leper Asylums
- Reformatory
- Central Laboratory
- Agricultural Experimental Station
- Grain Inspection Station
- Stud Farm
- Sheep Farm
- Forestry Experimental Station
- Fishery Experimental Station
- Bovine Infectious Disease Serum Factory
- Keijo Imperial University
- Government Schools and Colleges
- The Government-General Library
- Korea Taxation Petition Investigation Committee
- Forest Lands Survey Committee
- Korean Industrial Life Insurance Review Board
- Korean History Compilation Committee
- Maritime Tribunal
- Society for the Preservation of Precious Artifacts, Historic Sites, Scenic Places, and Natural Monuments

The number of officials also grew. Full-time employees (the so-called bureaucrats) were joined by contract and adjunct employees for a total workforce of about 25,000 people on the central government payroll in 1914. By 1937, that number had swelled to 65,000. Looking at just the bureaucrats, the Government-General of Korea is said to have become a giant ministry in the Japanese imperial government. For example, at the end of 1926, the Japanese imperial government employed a total of 148,000 bureaucrats, of whom 28,000 worked for the Government-General of Korea, making it the largest single entity within the government. The next largest entities were the Ministry of Communications (23,000) and the Ministry of Railways (21,000) (Okamoto 2008, 43–45). Because the Government-General of Korea was the central government of a large territory outside Japan, however, it is not really surprising that it employed more people than a domestic ministry. In Korea, the Communications Bureau was the counterpart agency to Japan's Ministry of Communications, and the Railway Bureau (which, as I note later, operated the railways except during 1918 to 1925, when operation was entrusted to the South Manchuria Railway Company) was the counterpart to the Ministry of Railways. It is not appropriate, therefore, to compare the Government-General of Korea as a whole, which contained these two bureaus, with the domestic ministries in Japan and say that the former was exceptionally large.

At the end of 1926, the ratio of central-government bureaucrats to total population was 100,000 to 60 million in Japan (or 1.7 bureaucrats per thousand) and 28,000 to 19 million in Korea (or 1.5 per thousand). The ratio in Korea was therefore slightly lower than in Japan. One must note, however, that these results vary from year to year and depend on how one defines the scope of the bureaucracy.

Direct Rule under Japanese Nationals
Looking at the officials in the Government-General of Korea by nationality, we see that Japanese consistently outnumbered Koreans. In 1937, for example, there were approximately 65,000 people employed by the Gov-

ernment-General, of whom 41,000 were Japanese and 24,000 were Korean. Most of the high-ranking officials, that is, *shin-ninkan* (minister-level officials appointed directly by the Emperor) and *choku-ninkan* (imperial appointees on the director-general, vice-minister, and bureau chief levels), and mid-level officials, that is, *so-ninkan* (officials on the division head level) were Japanese nationals. With the exception of Imperial Navy Admiral Saito Makoto, all of the governor-generals of Korea were Imperial Army generals. There were also many Japanese nationals who filled lower-level positions, that is, *han-ninkan* (junior officials on the division staff level) and *koin* (adjunct employees). Although there were some Korean nationals in high bureaucratic positions, nearly all of them were limited to ceremonial and dormant posts.

As in Japan, the bureau and division chiefs in charge of day-to-day administration were often graduates of the Faculty of Law at Tokyo Imperial University. Gradually, there was an increase in the number of Japanese bureaucrats who had spent considerable time in Korea, including some who started their careers there. As time went on, this group of experts on Korea increased its influence within governmental circles in Korea.

The large number of Japanese bureaucrats in Korea reflects Japan's practice of direct rule, which contrasts with British rule in India. The British model, often called "indirect rule," depended on a very small number of elite English officials overseeing a large number of Indian bureaucrats who ran the government. In contrast, the Dutch model in the East Indies from the nineteenth century represents a direct-rule approach similar to the Japanese model in Korea, with Dutch nationals giving way to more and more local officials filling low-level posts over time. Although a comparison of the methods used by the Great Powers to administer their colonies is a subject worth discussing fully, it far exceeds the scope of this book, so I will stop here.

2. The Search for Financial Autonomy: 1906 to 1936

Prior History: Megata Reform

In 1904, on the basis of the First Japan-Korea Convention, Megata Tanetaro (1853–1926), director-general of the Tax Bureau of the Ministry of Finance, was appointed as a financial adviser to the government of the Korean Empire. Megata, the son of a shogunal retainer, was so gifted that he attended Harvard Law School at a young age and obtained a degree there. He was one of many Japanese who entered the Korean government as administrative advisers. In 1907, after the Residency-General of Korea had been established, there were more than 400 Japanese advisers serving in the Korean government (Mizuta 1974b, 149).

When Megata was appointed, small-denomination coins, particularly copper coins issued by the Korean government, were the primary currency used by Koreans. Depending on the region, foreign (Japanese, Chinese, and Russian) coins and banknotes were also in circulation.

Regulations on public finance were not strictly implemented, so that each bureau and agency tended to make payments and collect taxes arbitrarily. In many cases, it was common practice for officials in both the central and regional governments to embezzle tax funds for personal use. Also, the budget of the Korean imperial household was part of the state budget.

Megata's first task was to correct chaotic currency circulation by undertaking the Currency Readjustment Project. He recovered the nickel coins that had been issued in excessive amounts by the Korean government in the 1890s and replaced them with coins identical to those used in Japan. He also officially authorized the universal validity of banknotes issued by Dai-Ichi Ginko, which had begun operating on the Korean Peninsula in the 1870s and was already issuing banknotes. Dai-Ichi Ginko was commissioned by the Korean government to assume sole responsibility for the Currency Readjustment Project's administrative work, thus becoming the de facto central bank of Korea (in 1909, the newly established Kankoku Ginko [renamed Chosen Ginko after annexation] took on these duties). As a result, the monetary systems in Korea and Japan became integrated.

Megata also reformed financial systems and institutions and worked to bolster the strict oversight of annual expenditures and regional tax collection. In addition, he prepared the way for cadastral surveys. Land taxes were the most important source of state revenue, and cadastral surveys were essential to standardize land tax collection. This need was recognized by the Korean government, which had made plans in the late 1890s to conduct cadastral surveys, but these plans were never implemented. Preparatory activities undertaken by Megata included the enactment of regulations, the establishment of relevant bureaus and departments, and technical training provided by Japanese surveyors.

Public Finance under the Residency-General:
Using Japanese Funds to Govern Korea

As previously mentioned, the Japanese government established the Residency-General of Korea in 1906, when it assumed supervisory control of Korea prior to annexation in 1910. At the time, the Korean government was saddled with substantial debt (about 2.4 million yen), which was called the "imperial household debt." This debt was domestic in nature and had begun to accrue before the abdication of Emperor Gojong in 1907. It included unpaid bills for purchased goods, construction work, and salaries connected with the imperial household. The settling of accounts was a serious concern, but following the policy of the Residency-General, the Korean government refused to pay many of its creditors and wrote off a large portion of the debt in 1909.

Prior to 1904, the Korean government owed very little to foreign creditors. Foreign debt began accumulating in 1905 with a loan of 3 million yen from Dai-Ichi Ginko, which was used to bolster financing for the Currency Readjustment Project. The Korean government also issued bonds in Tokyo to pay off existing domestic debt (2 million yen underwritten by Dai-Ichi Ginko, with a contract stipulating a three-year grace period and two-year redemption period). In addition, the Korean government borrowed 1.5 million yen from the Japanese government to finance the establishment of public financial institutions.

Subsequently, the Korean government borrowed more (from Japan and, to a lesser extent, Britain and France) to finance civil engineering projects, education, government-run enterprises, and the establishment of financial institutions. By the time of annexation, Korea's foreign debt had ballooned to around 46 million yen. What place did this debt occupy in the budget of the Korean government? Below, I explore this question for the years 1908 and 1909 (table 1-4).

In 1908, the Korean government had an annual revenue of about 22 million yen, of which 8.9 million, or about 40 percent, was derived from loans and public bonds. In 1909, loans and bonds accounted for 12 million yen, or about 42 percent, of the total annual revenue of 28 million yen. Most of the loans and bonds were financed in Japan, so that the Korean government was highly dependent on Japanese funds.

Land taxes accounted for the lion's share of total tax revenues. These were traditional taxes levied on agricultural land and paid by cultivators (including tenant farmers). In 1908, the Korean government reformed the system and adopted the principle of taxing landowners. Because the tax collection was badly administered, only 4 million yen was raised from land taxes in 1906 (compared to a budget of 5.2 million). After organizational reforms, revenues from land taxes increased rapidly, exceeding 6 million yen by 1908–1909. Tariffs were the next important source of tax revenue. After Korean ports were opened to foreign trade in 1876, revenue from this source (5 to 10 percent *ad valorem*) grew as trade developed.

On the spending side, the largest ordinary and extraordinary expenditures were incurred by the Home Affairs Department (equivalent to Japan's Ministry of Home Affairs) and the Finance Department (equivalent to Japan's Ministry of Finance) (table 1-5). A detailed examination reveals that, for the Home Affairs Department, regional policing was the largest ordinary expenditure and civil engineering projects such as road-building and waterworks construction were the largest extraordinary

Table 1-4.

Annual Revenue of the Korean Government, 1908–09

(1,000 yen)

	Taxes, government-run enterprises, and other ordinary revenue				Loans and bonds	Surplus from previous fiscal year	Total
	Land taxes	Tariffs	Other	Total			
1908	6,700	3,180	2,945	12,825	8,931	318	22,074
1909	6,337	3,007	4,532	13,876	11,991	2,599	28,466

Note: Year-end aggregate. Figures are rounded off to the nearest 1,000 yen so that the combined values in the columns do not necessarily match the totals shown.
Source: The Government-General of Korea 1911, *Chosen Sotokufu tokei nempo: Dai 4-ji*, 926–927.

Table 1-5.

Annual Expenditures of the Korean Government, 1908–09

A. Ordinary Expenditures

(1,000 yen)

	Imperial Household	Home Affairs Dept.	Finance Dept.	Defense Dept.	Justice Dept.	Education Dept.	Agriculture, Commerce and Industry Dept.	Total
1908	1,500	3,288	4,419	276	868	287	850	11,487
1909	1,676	3,982	6,314	148	1,366	394	924	14,804

B. Extraordinary Expenditures

	Home Affairs Dept.	Finance Dept.	Defense Dept.	Justice Dept.	Education Dept.	Agriculture, Commerce and Industry Dept.	Total
1908	2,747	3,582	729	60	199	328	7,645
1909	2,789	9,763	2	—	245	559	13,356

Note: Year-end aggregate. Figures are rounded so that the combined values in the columns do not necessarily match the totals shown.
Source: The Government-General of Korea 1911, *Chosen Sotokufu tokei nempo: Dai 4-ji*, 928–944.

expenditure. For the Finance Department, the largest ordinary expenditure was repaying the principal and interest on the government debt, while extraordinary expenditures included large sums for investment in financial institutions, loans, subsidies, and the construction of government office buildings and customs houses. Military expenditures were modest and dedicated to wrapping up the disbandment of the Korean military in 1907 (before disbandment, these expenditures were quite large). As these figures show, in 1908 and 1909, once expenses related to government debt are removed, the Korean government prioritized maintaining public safety and building infrastructure.

The Residency-General was distinct from the Korean government and was funded directly by the Japanese government through the Ministry of Finance. Its expenditures in 1908 and 1909 totaled approximately 7.1 million yen and 6.4 million yen, respectively. Large portions of these expenditures (5.3 million yen and 4.65 million yen, respectively) were earmarked as cash advances to the Korean government in the form of loans that bore no interest and had no set redemption period. These funds constituted most of the Korean government's annual revenue through foreign loans and bonds described earlier. In addition to expenditures for the Residency-General, the Japanese government spent large sums to cover the administrative and operating costs associated with governing Korea. One of the main uses for those funds was railway construction and repair. Massive military expenditures were also required to suppress anti-Japanese armed resistance in Korea. Total administrative, operational, and military spending (the so-called "Korean administrative costs"), including expenditures for the Residency-General, totaled about 31 million yen in 1908 and 21 million yen in 1909 (settled accounts). This represented about 4 to 5 percent of the total expenditures (settled accounts) in the general account of the Japanese government in 1908 (640 million yen) and 1909 (530 million yen).

The Account of the Government-General of Korea

After annexation, in September 1910, the Japanese government established a special account for the Government-General of Korea as part of the imperial state budget. Along with this measure, it eliminated the budgets of the Korean government and the Residency-General of Korea. The Korean government was not required to repay the 13.28 million yen in advances and 1.5 million yen in loans (bonds) that the Japanese government had provided.

The main sources of revenue for the Government-General were taxes, revenue from government-run enterprises, subsidies, and government bonds. The subsidies came out of the general account of the Japanese government, which also issued bonds for the Government-General of Korea. The largest revenue stream from government-run enterprises came from the railways (except for the years 1918–1924). Other revenue sources included the postal service, telecommunications, and monopolies (after 1921). Before annexation, the Japanese government owned and operated the Kankoku Tetsudo (Korean Railway) and managed its finances through a special account in the state budget. In 1911, most of that account was folded into the special account of the Government-General of Korea. In that year, railway revenue accounted for over 20 percent of all ordinary revenues in the special account of the Government-General of Korea. That railway revenue, however, was not profit because the huge costs involved in running the railway were included on the expenditure side, so that it cannot be said that government-run railways contributed substantially to the financial solvency of the Government-General.

In the following analysis, I first examine changes in annual revenue from taxes, subsidies, and bonds, putting aside the revenue from government-run enterprises. In response to the Banzai Sojo Incident in March 1919, a transition was made from *budan seiji* (a government based on military force) to *bunka seiji* (one based on the gentler concept of cultural governance). Therefore, I divide my analysis into two periods: the 1910s, and the period from 1920 to 1936.

Annual Revenue: Japanese Funds and Taxes
1910s

In 1911, the Government-General received a subsidy equivalent to tax revenues and furthermore procured funds from government bonds in Japan (table 1-6). Immediately after annexation, the administration of Korea thus depended on Japanese financing as it had under the Residency-General of Korea.

The first task before the Government-General was to make Korea financially self-sufficient, which meant increasing tax revenues so that the subsidy from the Japanese general account could be reduced. In the case of Taiwan, another Japanese colony, a similar subsidy had been eliminated within ten years from the establishment of Japanese imperial rule. The Government-General of Taiwan had rich revenue sources that

Table 1-6.

Annual Revenue of the Government-General of Korea: Taxes, Subsidies, and Bonds, 1911–1919

(1,000 yen)

	Taxes			Subsidies	Bonds
	Total				
		Land taxes	Tariffs		
1911	12,441	6,648	4,062	12,350	10,000
1912	13,362	6,703	4,712	12,350	14,900
1913	13,904	6,980	4,807	10,000	11,103
1914	16,685	10,101	3,893	9,000	7,641
1915	17,494	10,051	4,416	8,000	8,945
1916	18,876	10,059	5,032	7,000	10,585
1917	22,679	10,226	7,295	5,000	12,830
1918	29,185	11,569	10,389	3,000	13,098
1919	38,519	11,178	15,546	—	14,435

Note: The figures are settled amounts for each fiscal year, with tax totals including land taxes, tariffs, and other taxes (not shown). Figures in the "Bonds" column include funds borrowed to finance enterprises or projects.
Source: Ministry of Finance 1958, chap. 1, appended table.

made this possible, including land taxes, a consumption tax on sugar, and monopoly sales of opium, camphor, tobacco, and salt. Similar results were anticipated in Korea.

In 1914, the Government-General of Korea revised the Land Tax Ordinance to increase land taxes. Revenues from land taxes had remained virtually unchanged before and after annexation, but this revision raised them by approximately 40 percent. Cadastral surveys were completed in 1918, thereby identifying landowners (who were responsible for paying land taxes) throughout Korea and establishing the value of the land owned. In the same year, the Government-General comprehensively revised the Land Tax Ordinance and set the tax rate at 1.3 percent of land value. This rate was designed to keep the tax amount unchanged. Taxes had been drastically raised four years earlier, so the Government-General sought to avoid a further increase by calculating a tax rate that would yield existing revenue. Concerning tariffs, the Japanese government announced both at home and abroad at the time of annexation that Korea's existing tariff system would be left unchanged for a period of ten years. Therefore, the basic tariff framework was maintained throughout the 1910s, and tariff revenue increased in tandem with the expansion of trade. As tax revenues increased, the subsidy paid by the Japanese government was reduced year by year until it was finally eliminated completely in 1919.

As early as 1911, the Imperial Diet passed the Government Bonds for Korean Public Works Act. As the title indicated, these were not so-called deficit bonds intended to cover a shortfall in general expenses; rather, they were earmarked for specific enterprises or projects. Limits were also placed on the total amount of bonds that could be issued. The main purpose of the bonds was to build physical infrastructure in Korea, with particular emphasis on constructing and repairing the railways.

1920–1936

The Banzai Sojo Incident in 1919 was a great shock to the Japanese government as well as the Government-General of Korea, and it sparked a reassessment of the strong-arm rule over Korea after annexation. By adopting gentler policies, they tried to appease the Korean population and restore social stability. Specific measures included the relaxation of restrictions on publications, assembly, and personal association; expansion of the scope of Koreans appointed to governmental posts; and reform of the police system. Before these reforms, the Japanese had used a gendarmerie police system, and military police officers sent from Japan had performed police duties together with civilian police officers. The reforms did away with the military component and gave policing responsibility exclusively to civilian police officers. To effect the reform, it was necessary to increase the number of civilian police officers substantially. The cost associated with reforming the administration of the police and other governmental departments exceeded the scope of what could be collected in taxes. After 1920, therefore, the Government-General once again began receiving a subsidy from the general account of the Japanese government.

As in the 1910s, the main sources of tax revenue in the 1920s were land taxes and tariffs. However, the prominence of these two sources gradually declined (table 1-7). The land tax rate was raised to 1.7 percent in 1922, but it was lowered to 1.6 percent in 1934 when a tax on individual income (discussed later in this chapter) was introduced. It was lowered yet again in the following year to 1.5 percent.

In 1920, the grace period for reviewing tariffs expired. Because Korea had become a part of the Japanese Empire, there was no due cause to impose tariffs on goods traded between Korea and Japan. Therefore, in Japan, tariffs levied on most imported Korean goods were immediately eliminated. In Korea, however, the elimination of tariffs on imported Japanese goods would have left a large hole in the Government-General's annual revenue, so those tariffs were maintained. Efforts were subsequently made to reduce them, but they were not completely eliminated until 1940. The focus of the tariff issue gradually shifted from revenue to protection for Korean industry (especially the textile industry). After the liquor tax rate was increased in 1916, revenue from this source

Table 1-7.

Annual Revenue of the Government-General of Korea:
Taxes, Subsidies, and Bonds, 1920–36

(1,000 yen)

	Taxes					Subsidies	Bonds
	Total						
		Land taxes	Tariffs	Liquor taxes	Income taxes		
1920	34,840	11,453	9,748	3,768	1,599	10,000	22,356
1921	36,891	11,647	13,323	5,154	832	15,000	37,220
1922	42,525	15,201	13,825	8,505	1,089	15,600	21,126
1923	34,393	15,226	7,145	7,750	954	15,017	6,595
1924	37,396	14,894	8,230	8,335	1,052	15,021	9,000
1925	38,629	15,254	9,926	8,424	827	16,569	9,000
1926	41,947	15,349	12,203	9,460	1,091	19,761	13,383
1927	43,363	15,436	9,949	11,223	1,212	15,425	18,373
1928	44,633	14,571	10,420	12,860	1,341	15,458	17,820
1929	45,988	14,820	10,717	13,230	1,200	15,423	13,748
1930	43,479	15,617	8,466	12,322	1,135	15,474	12,506
1931	40,392	15,810	7,401	11,248	763	15,474	13,214
1932	41,166	15,422	7,966	11,366	1,007	12,914	14,035
1933	47,625	15,854	11,158	13,529	1,325	12,854	25,648
1934	56,129	14,738	12,728	16,584	5,114	12,825	27,926
1935	64,802	13,768	13,266	19,590	9,202	12,826	20,923
1936	75,392	13,313	16,814	21,756	12,239	12,918	26,122

Note: The figures are settled amounts for each fiscal year, with tax totals including taxes not shown.
Sources: Ministry of Finance 1958, chap. 1, appended table; and The Government-General of Korea 1922–1938, *Chosen Sotokufu tokei nempo*.

steadily rose. Eventually the liquor tax surpassed land taxes and tariffs as a source of revenue.

In 1916, the Japanese corporate income tax act was applied in Korea and the earnings of Korean companies began to be taxed. At that time, many companies in Korea were owned by Japanese nationals. For the sake of fairness, it was necessary to maintain parity in the amount of taxes levied on companies operating in Japan and Korea. In 1920, Korea's own income tax ordinance was promulgated. This, too, targeted companies but not individuals. In 1926, the Government-General established a tax commission charged with creating basic tax policy. Some of the main provisions of the new tax code included establishing a general income tax as the main pillar of the taxation, supplemented by various revenue taxes (levied at a flat rate according to the size of the business) and indirect taxes such as commodity and service taxes and tariffs, and expanding tax collection agencies. Following this policy, the first step for the Government-General was to levy two kinds of revenue tax in 1927: a business tax and a tax on capital interest. In 1934, the tax system underwent a radical reform with the introduction of an individual income tax and an inheritance tax. At the same time, tax offices and taxation supervision offices were established in the central administration. The tasks of levying and collecting national taxes were transferred to these new agencies from the regional agencies that had carried them out before. With the reform of the tax system and the establishment of collection agencies, tax revenues grew in 1935–36 to an amount that was double that of the government subsidy and bonds combined. Even then, the income tax accounted for less than 20 percent of the total tax revenues, leaving the goal of making the income tax the central pillar of the tax system unachieved.

Annual Expenditures:
General Expenditures, Expenditures for Maintaining Public Order,
Expenditures for Government-Run Enterprises,
and Expenditures for Servicing Debt

I examine total expenditures in three categories: general expenditures, expenditures for government-run enterprises, and expenditures for servicing debt. As I did when analyzing revenue, I look at data from two discrete time periods, the 1910s and 1920–1936.

General expenditures are defined as the working expenses for running the government. The expenditures for maintaining public order as a component of this category are particularly noteworthy. Maintaining public order is the first duty of government. How much did the Government-General spend on maintaining public order in the Korean Peninsula, where non-Japanese people lived? I define expenditures for maintaining public order as the total amounts calculated by the Government-General to cover policing and judicial costs (called "court" and "prison" costs prior to 1936). Expenditures for government-run enterprises include operational expenses and costs associated with building and maintaining infrastructure. Those for servicing debt include amounts paid into a special account of the national debt consolidation fund in the Japanese government; these funds represented repayment of principle and interest on bonds issued for the Government-General of Korea.

1910s

In 1911, expenditures totaled about 49 million yen, of which 37 million (76%) were general expenditures and 10 million yen (20%) were for government-run enterprises (table 1-8). Subsequently, total expenditures and general expenditures increased annually, becoming 1.6 and 1.3 times larger, respectively, by 1919. The rate of increase was even higher for expenditures for government-run enterprises, reaching 44 percent of total expenditures by 1917. Most of that was associated with the railways, including operating expenses (personnel and supplies) and construction and improvement expenses. In August of 1917, the Government-General of Korea entrusted operation of the railways to the South Manchuria Railway Company. Railway operations were therefore eliminated from government expenditures beginning in 1918, although construction and improvement expenses remained. As a result, the proportion of expenditures accounted for by government-run enterprises declined. Even so, they still accounted for 30 percent of total expenditures in 1919.

Expenditures for maintaining public order constituted less than 20 percent of general expenditures in 1911, a proportion that did not change significantly in the following years. During this period, the Government-General was financially responsible not only for ordinary police but also military police involved in civilian police activities (including personnel expenses for Korean assistants). In 1912, there were 5,735 civilian police officers in Korea, of whom 2,594 were Japanese and 3,141 Korean. There were also 7,769 military police officers, of whom 4,473 were Korean assistants, indicating that many Koreans were involved in policing under Japanese rule.

Table 1-8.

Annual Expenditures of the Government-General of Korea, 1911–19

(1,000 yen)

	Total	General expenditures		Government-run enterprises	Servicing debt
		Total	Maintaining public order		
1911	48,741	36,940	6,551	10,068	1,733
1912	52,892	39,517	6,750	10,988	2,387
1913	57,989	40,735	7,055	12,137	5,117
1914	59,412	31,528	6,715	22,683	5,201
1915	58,873	30,304	6,672	22,168	6,401
1916	59,848	30,870	6,815	23,967	5,011
1917	62,642	30,075	6,660	27,097	5,470
1918	65,141	35,877	7,453	21,590	7,674
1919	77,560	46,961	8,369	24,567	6,032

Note: The figures are the budget amounts for each fiscal year, and they are rounded down to the nearest 1,000 yen.
Source: The Government-General of Korea 1999, (2), 693–695.

1920–1936

Although total expenditures and general expenditures decreased in some years during this period, they still showed long-term growth (table 1-9). As a result, total annual expenditures in 1936 were six times higher than the level of the early years after annexation, and general expenditures were three times higher. The fastest growing expenditure categories were government-run enterprises and debt servicing. In 1925, railway operating expenditures were returned to the budget when responsibility for railway operations was transferred back from the South Manchuria Railway Company. This contributed to a substantial increase in expenditures for government-run enterprises in that year, which surpassed the amount of general expenditures. Subsequently, outlays for the operation, construction, and improvement of railways in Korea continued to rise, so that expenditures for government-run enterprises were 1.5 times higher than expenditures for general purposes in 1936 and accounted for 54 percent of total expenditures (railway-related outlays accounted for about 65 percent of total expenditures for government-run enterprises in that year).

Expenditures for servicing debt also increased throughout this period as more bonds were issued. Those for maintaining public order more than doubled between 1919 and 1920 as a result of increases in personnel, exceeding 30 percent of general expenditures in 1920. Another substantial increase occurred in 1921, after which it remained virtually unchanged over the long term. As a result, the proportion of general expenditures accounted for by the maintenance of public order dropped from 36 percent in 1921 to 25 percent in 1936.

Local Public Finance

There were four kinds of local government in Korea: provinces (*do*), cities (*fu*), towns (*yu*), and villages (*men*). Provinces were equivalent to prefectures in Japan but generally larger (Korea had a total of 13 provinces). The system of *fu* and *men* was officially adopted in 1914. In 1931, *men* with large populations were reclassified as *yu*.

Table 1-9.

Annual Expenditures of the Government-General of Korea, 1920–36

(1,000 yen)

	Total	General expenditures		Government-run enterprises	Servicing debt
		Total	Maintaining public order		
1920	114,316	73,305	22,736	33,570	7,441
1921	162,474	84,247	29,871	68,742	9,485
1922	158,993	88,640	29,227	57,653	12,700
1923	146,007	81,969	29,219	51,241	12,797
1924	142,760	83,836	29,969	45,356	13,568
1925	178,082	77,427	27,024	86,056	14,599
1926	194,487	85,104	26,991	94,263	15,120
1927	210,910	91,935	27,799	102,158	16,817
1928	222,746	93,431	28,606	111,699	17,616
1929	246,852	104,476	29,676	122,929	19,447
1930	239,729	95,176	29,350	121,028	23,525
1931	238,923	94,178	28,079	120,038	24,707
1932	220,140	89,882	27,310	107,169	23,089
1933	232,026	95,341	27,246	112,052	24,633
1934	274,634	116,821	28,567	132,650	25,163
1935	290,267	115,258	29,869	147,982	27,027
1936	329,645	119,811	30,837	178,822	31,012

Note: The figures are the budget amounts for each fiscal year and are rounded off to the nearest 1,000 yen. In 1936, a new expenditure category was added: transportation and telecommunications, after which outlays for government-run enterprises decreased dramatically. In this table, all of the expenditures placed in the new category are assumed to have previously been in the government-run enterprises category, so the two amounts have been combined and listed as expenditures for government-run enterprises.

Sources: The Government-General of Korea 1999, (2), 693–695; (3), 518.

Local governments performed general public administrative duties, with the exception of primary education, which was handled by two separate administrative organizations: *gakko kumiai* and *gakkohi*. Basically, the former was for Japanese students, and the latter for Korean students. The *gakko kumiai* was financed by association fees, and the *gakkohi* was funded by dues levied on those entering school. This revenue was combined with subsidies and other funds to operate schools. In 1931, the *gakko kumiai* and *gakkohi* were abolished within *fu*, and their duties were transferred to the First Special Economy and Second Special Economy.

In 1915, the combined budgets of all the local governments in Korea totaled only about 10 million yen, but they expanded rapidly in the following years, reaching 140 million yen by 1935 (table 1-10). Initially, most of their annual revenue came from taxes (e.g., a surtax on land), but that proportion steadily declined thereafter because of increases in subsidies from the Government-General and loans. Most of the expenditures of local governments were directed toward general administration and sectors related to local life and industry. An example for 1934 is shown in table 1-11.

3. The Development of Governance: What Did the Government-General Achieve?

The Significance of the Cadastral Survey

After annexation, the Government-General of Korea immediately set about conducting a cadastral survey, which became the foundation for the equitable assessment and collection of land taxes. Many scholars advocating the theory of colonial exploitation have strongly criticized the cadastral survey because it purportedly resulted in many Korean farmers losing their land. According to these scholars, the farmers were not used to filling out forms and were sometimes not even informed

Table 1-10.

Annual Revenue of Regional Governments, 1915–35

(1,000 yen)

	Provinces		Cities		Towns and villages		Gakko kumiai	Gakkohi	Grand total
	Total	Taxes	Total	Taxes	Total	Taxes			
1915	3,367	1,462	1,958	622	2,856	2,249	1,318	1,151	10,650
1920	16,702	8,628	3,749	1,676	11,917	9,553	4,354	8,144	44,866
1925	26,316	11,687	8,103	2,203	17,882	11,335	5,753	13,314	71,368
1930	36,782	18,310	12,039	2,703	21,573	13,484	6,072	15,297	91,763
1935	71,654	21,338	24,136	5,404	25,790	14,690	3,813	18,133	143,526

Note: The figures are the settled amounts for each fiscal year and rounded off to the nearest 1,000 yen. The grand totals include the totals for all types of regional government plus gakko kumiai and gakkohi.
Source: The Government-General of Korea, *Chosen Sotokufu tokei nempo* (each relevant year).

Table 1-11.

Annual Expenditures of Regional Governments: Main Outlays and Totals, 1934

(1,000 yen)

Provinces		Cities		Towns and villages	
Industrial development and business promotion	19,213	Education	5,839	Administration	12,701
Civil engineering	17,883	Civil engineering	3,219	Civil engineering	1,746
Education and social programs	15,166	Waterworks	1,714	Industrial development	1,725
Total	70,524	Total	20,881	Total	24,602

Note: The figures for provinces are the settled amounts; the others are budget amounts. The total exceeds the sum of the listed expenditures because not all categories are shown.
Source: The Government-General of Korea 1944, 378–386.

that the survey was occurring, and therefore they failed to submit the documents certifying landownership. Undocumented land and public commons were claimed by the state and later sold to people influential both in and outside the communities in question (including Japanese and the traditional Korean land-owning class).

Recent research, however, has clearly shown this interpretation of events to be mistaken: the survey did not in fact cause many Korean farmers to lose their land (Lee 2009, 79–85). Cadastral surveys represent an attempt to stimulate economic growth in societies based on private ownership. As such, they are an essential task for any government. The Government-General of Korea assigned large amounts of official funds and personnel to this project over the years, and this achievement should be recognized as a large step toward the modernization of Korea.

A Low Tax Burden Ratio

The tax system in Korea centered on land taxes formulated on the basis of the cadastral survey. Additional revenue was obtained from indirect taxes, such as tariffs and a liquor tax, and various revenue taxes. Although progress was made on levying income taxes, there were limits to expanding it. Generally, it is difficult to adopt a tax system centered on an income tax in less developed countries because the government lacks the administrative ability to capture personal income (even though it may be able to keep track of corporate income). In any case, most households are too poor and ill-equipped to pay it. Korea was no exception.

The tax burden ratio (the ratio between gross tax revenue and national income) indicates the degree of the tax burden placed on residents. Among prewar Korea, Taiwan, and Japan, the tax burden ratio was highest in Japan, followed by Taiwan and Korea (table 1-12). In other words, of the three regions, the tax burden ratio was lowest in Korea.

This was hardly surprising. Korea's per capita gross national product was only 30 to 40 percent that of Japan, and 60 to 70 percent that of Taiwan. Officials in charge of the public finance of the Government-General of Korea fully understood that Koreans had little ability to pay taxes.

They plainly stated that, because Korea was economically backward compared to Japan, they set the rates of income tax, liquor tax, and other taxes at a level lower than those in Japan (Mizuta 1974a, 137–138). Because of this, subsidies and government bonds constituted an indispensable part of the budget, keeping Korea's finances dependent on Japan. From the Japanese perspective, the financial burden of administrating Korea was an ongoing expense item (besides subsidies, the cost of maintaining the Japanese garrison force in Korea was paid out of the general account of the central government).

The Government-General of Korea as a Corporate Entity

The expenditures of the Government-General of Korea and the local governments grew in every area. The expansion of the government's role (the transition from a cheap government to an expensive one) is a common trait among modern nations. In this sense, the Government-General of Korea developed in the same way as other governments of modern states.

From a financial perspective, the most important duty for the Government-General was operating government enterprises, with a particular focus on the railways. Responsibility for railway operation was temporarily entrusted to the South Manchuria Railway Company, but even then, the Government-General continued to be responsible for formulating operational plans and covering the costs of building and

Table 1-12.

Tax Burden Ratios in Korea, Taiwan, and Japan

(%)

	Korea	Taiwan	Japan
1911–15	3.9	9.6	13.1
1916–20	3.9	7.7	9.1
1921–25	5.0	8.4	11.2
1926–30	6.2	8.5	11.3
1931–35	7.6	9.0	10.5

Note: The figures represent an annual average of the indicated time periods. Figures for Korea and Taiwan are calculated by dividing national tax revenues, local tax revenues, and monopoly profits by gross domestic expenditure; figures for Japan are calculated by dividing the same revenues by gross national expenditure.
Source: Kimura 1989, 295.

improving new and old lines. In light of this, the Government-General of Korea was not merely an administrative agency, but in fact a large-scale corporate entity. Throughout the period covered in this chapter, the railways operated in the black, but the profits they earned were lower than the interest payments that had to be made on borrowed funds (Hirai 1997, 154). Overall, then, the railway business was unprofitable, but because the railways were essential for the governance and development of Korea, the Government-General continued to operate them.

Stabilization of Public Order

All suzerain states must confront the vital issue of maintaining public order in their colonies. Expenditures on public safety increased in Korea after the Banzai Sojo Incident in 1919, but they subsequently remained stable through the mid-1930s. This lack of increase reflects the fact that no anti-Japanese movements comparable in size to the Banzai Sojo Incident occurred during that period. The Government-General of Korea did not choose to strengthen its rule on the basis of military force or fear (involving such techniques as use of concentration camps and a widespread, dense network of secret police). Instead, it transitioned to gentler policies that enabled it to control anti-Japanese movements. Why was that? This question has almost never been asked, but it is surely a question of deep interest in the field of Korean historical research. Finding an answer will require a multidisciplinary approach that may include ethnology and colonial social psychology.

The Development of Modern Industry

Rapid Departure from Agriculture

Korea lacked modern industry when it was annexed by Japan. How did the Korean economy change under Japanese rule? Changes in industrial structure in Korea clearly indicate economic transformation. According to recent estimates, agriculture, forestry, and fishery (as calculated by the amount of value added) accounted for approximately 70 percent of gross domestic product (GDP) in 1912 (table 2-1). This percentage declined decade by decade to about 40 in 1939. In less than 30 years, then, traditional primary industry (mostly agriculture) shrank to less than half the total economy in terms of the value of products. Conversely, the combined proportion of mining and manufacturing industries in the total economy grew significantly, from about 5 percent to about 20 percent during the same period.

In this chapter I first examine changes in the agricultural sector and then evaluate the mining and manufacturing sector from annexation in 1910 until the late 1930s. Later development through the collapse of the Japanese Empire will be discussed in chapter 4.

Table 2-1.

Proportion of Total GDP by Industry (based on nominal prices)

(%)

	Agriculture, forestry, and fishery	Mining and manufacturing	Electricity, gas, and construction	Services
1912	68.1	4.9	1.9	25.1
1920	61.8	7.4	2.7	28.1
1930	49.0	9.4	6.3	35.3
1939	41.1	18.6	9.1	31.3

Note: Figures show a three-year average centered on the indicated year.
Source: Kim Nak-nyeon 2008, 315.

1. Agriculture

Growth of Production and Expansion of the Money Economy

While the agriculture, forestry, and fishery sector shrank in relation to other sectors, its production increased. From 1912 to 1939, agricultural production (in terms of real value added) rose by an average of 1.9 percent annually (Kim Nak-nyeon 2008, 406, table I-6). During the same period, agricultural products in Japan grew at a much lower rate, 1.0 percent (Ohkawa, Takamatsu, and Yamamoto 1987, 228, table 26).

The coverage of the original statistics issued by the Government-General of Korea in the 1910s was limited. Therefore, estimates of the growth rate of Korean agricultural products from 1910 through 1919 are based on many assumptions that might result in overestimation. Even when we disregard this early period and limit our assessment to 1920 through 1939, however, we still find a high average annual growth rate of 1.5 percent. Such rapid growth is rarely found elsewhere unless a vast area of new land is being cleared or a large labor surplus is available.

Rice accounted for the largest proportion of total agricultural output in value. Throughout the period of Japanese rule, rice accounted for more than 40 percent of total output almost every year, with a peak of 54 percent occurring in 1934.

Rice Production

In the early 1910s, the annual amount of rice produced in Korea stood at around 12 million *koku* (1 *koku* of brown rice is about 150 kg). It subsequently grew rapidly, reaching 27 million *koku* by 1937. Since cultivated land area increased less than 15 percent during that period, the increase in production is mainly attributable to greater productivity per unit area. By 1937, production per *tan* (about 10 ares, 1 are = 100 m^2) had reached 1.6 *koku*, an increase of more than 80 percent compared with the beginning of the period. Geographically, the largest gains in productivity accrued in northern Korea. Because of the added factor of expanded cultivated area in this region, rice production in northern Korea grew more sharply.

Improved Varieties of Rice

In 1906, before annexation, the Residency-General of Korea established the Research Station of Model Agriculture (which later became an Agricultural Experimental Farm) in Suwon, near Seoul, where research on the selective breeding of rice was conducted. Satellite stations and seed nurseries were also established throughout Korea. After annexation, the Government-General selected superior varieties from these facilities, distributed them to farmers free of charge, and provided guidance on cultivation methods for them.

The main varieties selected at the time included *Wase-shinriki* (originally from Kumamoto Prefecture; features high yields even with little fertilizer; also known as *So-shinriki*); *Kokuryo-miyako* (originally from Yamaguchi Prefecture; high-quality rice well-suited to the manufacture of sake); and *Tama-nishiki* (originally from Tochigi Prefecture; high-quality rice featuring drought resistance).

At the time of annexation, the dissemination rate of these improved varieties of rice in Korea was virtually nil. Subsequent dissemination occurred quickly, however, exceeding 50 percent by 1920. In that year, improved varieties accounted for 62 percent of the total output of rice.

It is said that the Government-General went so far as to mobilize police officers to disseminate the improved rice varieties. However, such rapid dissemination could not have been achieved solely through governmental guidance (or "coercion"). At the time, the established governmental organization was neither strong nor systematic enough to implement such a program throughout Korea. Therefore, the rapid dissemination that did occur can only be explained by a positive response on the part of local producers. Compared with native ones, the improved varieties of rice from Japan afforded Korean farmers higher incomes. In addition to higher yields and more stable crops, the superior quality of the new varieties commanded higher prices in the rice market.

Active Participation of Korean Farmers

Tenant farming was already widespread in Korea before Japan came on the scene. In the 1910s, about 70 percent of all farming households were either combined owner/tenant farmers or pure tenant farmers, with about half of the arable land area cultivated by tenant farmers. Nearly 70 percent of all rice paddies were cultivated by tenant farmers.

Many Korean landowners were reportedly absentee landlords who had no interest in managing their farm and did not even live in local villages. Before annexation, the actual work of running some of the farms fell to Japanese who lived in Korea. They bought Korean land and leased it to tenant farmers to cultivate crops, with an emphasis on rice. In the rice belt of southern Korea, there were Japanese individuals and companies who owned anywhere from several hundred to several thousand hectares of rice fields. The largest company of this type was Toyo Takushoku Kabushiki Kaisha (The Oriental Development Company), a semi-national enterprise of the Japanese Empire founded in 1908. It was only natural that these Japanese landowners would be first to adopt the improved varieties of rice. Their main objective was to maximize their income by exporting the rice they collected as rent from tenants to the home market in Japan.

Even as late as 1920, however, Japanese living in Korea owned only about 10 percent of the total cultivated rice area in Korea. This fact suggests that Koreans also played a part in widely disseminating improved varieties of rice. In addition, the money economy was growing rapidly at this time. Korean farmers had a strong incentive to acquire cash as manufactured goods entered Korea from Japan, taxes and other governmental fees were levied, and commercial fertilizers came on the market. In Korea, rice was by far the most important cash crop. Therefore, it hardly comes as a surprise that once Korean farmers understood the advantages of growing improved varieties of rice as a means to earn cash, they would naturally make the transition to those improved varieties. Whether the impetus came from the landowners or the tenant farmers may have depended on particular circumstances. In either case, Koreans responded to market opportunities newly opened to them.

This response to market opportunities was not limited to Korea.

The same phenomenon can be found in many parts of Asia and Africa in the nineteenth and twentieth centuries. In Southeast Asia such as Burma, Thailand, and Indochina, rice production burgeoned with the expansion of the export market. In those cases, so-called peasants who were seeking to gain cash transitioned from traditional rice cultivation for self-support to expanded commercial rice production (Myint 1981, 38–43).

There were, however, notable differences. These regions had large undeveloped areas, and the increase in rice production depended on the cultivation of newly cleared land. During that time, productivity per unit area declined. One reason for this decline was that no changes occurred either in the varieties of rice being grown or in cultivation methods. Also, clearing operations started with fertile land with a good water supply and gradually expanded to land with less and less advantageous characteristics (Wickizer and Bennett 1958, 256; Watanabe 1978, 37–43).

In short, Korea was a special case because the development of the money economy not only led to increased cash crop production but also triggered a change in cultivation methods (as was also the case in Taiwan under Japanese rule). As a result, Korean farmers showed a more active and innovative response to market opportunities than did farmers in Southeast Asia.

Increased Input of Fertilizer and Sanmai Zoshoku Keikaku

Research on improved varieties of rice was pursued continuously. In the late 1930s, *Ginbozu* was the most commonly planted variety in southern Korea. This was a high-yielding variety introduced from the Hokuriku region in northwestern Japan.

In northern Korea, a variety called *Rikuu no. 132* that originated in Akita Prefecture was widely planted. It was not only high-yielding but resistant to cold-weather damage and blight. It is well known that Miyazawa Kenji, a famous farmer and poet, provided agricultural guidance in the Tohoku region of northeastern Japan where cold-weather damage was almost an annual event. He worked diligently to disseminate this variety, which was also deemed delicious and highly prized in the marketplace (and is the forerunner of today's *Koshihikari* and *Sasanishiki* varieties).

Most improved varieties of rice required large amounts of fertilizer, and the consumption of fertilizer in Korea increased significantly under Japanese rule. This included self-supplied fertilizer (green manure, compost, etc.) and commercial fertilizer (fishmeal, oil cake, chemical fertilizer, etc.). Consumption of ammonium sulfate (a type of nitrogenous fertilizer) in particular increased in the 1930s. This development was closely related to the construction of modern fertilizer factories in Korea, as discussed below. Despite these advances, far less fertilizer was used by ordinary farmers in Korea than was used by farmers in Japan, even in the 1930s.

In 1920, the Government-General initiated the Sanmai Zoshoku Keikaku (Rice Production Development Program), with the purported goals of meeting growing demand for rice in Korea, boosting the economies of farming families, and contributing to a solution to food shortage problems in the Japanese Empire. The program set the ambitious goal of pursuing land improvement policies (improving irrigation, converting land use, and clearing new fields) and improving agricultural practices as a whole to increase annual rice production by 9.2 million *koku* (an increase of 60 percent compared with 1920) within fifteen years. Implementation did not proceed as planned, however, primarily for three reasons: rising prices inflated construction costs, interest rates on anticipated loans were higher than expected, and the special corporation slated to serve as the implementing agency was never formed.

The Government-General started over with a revised program implemented in 1926. Like its predecessor, it was ambitious, with the goal of increasing annual rice production by 8.2 million *koku* in fourteen years. The content of the revised program, however, was more refined, calling for direct government intervention to arrange large amounts of low-interest funding for land improvement and the purchase of fertilizer.

The program also established two land improvement agencies: Chosen Tochi Kairyo Kabushiki Kaisha (Korea Land Improvement Company, a half-public, half-private entity) and a land improvement division within Toyo Takushoku. Starting in the 1930s, farmers in Japan who were suffering economically from a serious recession strengthened their opposition to the importation of Korean rice. This made it necessary to reduce the goals of the revised program to increase Korean rice production and resulted in the dissolution of the two aforementioned land improvement agencies.

There is much debate concerning the political background, significance, results, and economic impact of the Sanmai Zoshoku Keikaku. Although I do not explore it in detail here, I will simply point out that rice production in Korea increased from about 14 million *koku* to 18–19 million *koku* between the years 1920–21 and 1931–32.

Sanmai Zoshoku Keikaku is considered to be the first large-scale agricultural development plan in the Japanese Empire (Tohata and Ohkawa 1935, 12). It was formulated and implemented by the Government-General, indicating that the latter was not simply an administrative organ, but also a large corporate entity that promoted the development of rice production as an industry.

Complementary Policies Pursued by the Government-General

Quality assurance is critically important if a cash crop is to be well-received in the market, and the Government-General made serious efforts in this area as well. In its unimproved state, Korean rice had many defects, such as incomplete dryness and contamination by husks, straw, dirt, and *akamai* (an old wild variety of red-colored rice). For this reason, Japanese rice distributors were autonomously conducting grain inspections in open ports even before annexation.

In 1915, the Government-General promulgated regulations that placed rice inspection under provincial authority. In 1917, the regulations were revised so that inspections were paid out of provincial budgets. In 1932, the additional step was taken of opening grain inspection centers and making the inspection of rice for export a national operation. Concerning packaging, the Government-General in 1927 issued *kamasu* (straw bag) inspection regulations designed to improve bag quality and ensure uniformity. In 1932, specifications for standardized straw bags were established.

The Government-General also promoted rice storage operations. Rice sales tended to be concentrated in the fall and winter after harvest, during which time lower prices were unavoidable. Modern storage facilities were necessary both in rice-producing regions and at ports where rice was loaded, both to maintain rice quality and to extend the selling period. In 1930, the Government-General announced a plan to construct rice storage facilities in Korea, which formed the basis for the establishment of Chosen Beikoku Soko Kabushiki Kaisha (Korea Rice Storehouse Company). The purpose of the company was to construct and operate "commercial" rice storehouses at ports and "agricultural" rice storehouses in rice-producing regions, as well as providing low-interest financing secured by stored rice. Under the plan, construction of the commercial rice storehouses proceeded rapidly; by 1933, they had a combined capacity of 1.6 million *koku*.

Before harvested rice reaches consumers, it must be husked and polished. This processing was done by private companies, and the Government-General was not directly involved in this process until the latter stages of World War II. The issue of processing rice is explored in a later section discussing manufacturing industries.

Stagnation in the Production of Other Food Crops

Under Japanese rule, production of barley, millet, and soybeans, which were the main dry-field food crops, stagnated because of the low dissemination rate of improved varieties and a decline in productivity per unit area. The Government-General showed little interest in non-rice food crops. It did not formulate a field improvement plan until 1931, and even then, it was much smaller in scale than the plan formulated for rice.

Soybeans were useful to farmers as a cash crop. The native soybeans cultivated in Korea were already of a high quality and were liked in Japan as raw material for producing tofu, miso, and soy sauce. They were even preferred over the well-known soybeans grown in Manchuria. In the second half of the 1910s, the export of Korean soybeans increased dramatically (from 500,000 *koku* in 1914 to 1.3 million *koku* in 1919). This reflects the influence of World War I, when the soybean market exploded. Exports remained at a high level in subsequent years, to the point where exports represented 20–30 percent of total Korean soybean output by the 1930s. If soybeans were a good cash crop, why did production not increase as the money economy developed in Korea? Regional observation reveals that, while soybean production declined in southern Korea in the 1920s and 1930s, it increased slightly in northern Korea. It is not easy to ascertain the reasons for this relative waxing and waning between regions, but it may be because farmers in northern Korea, responding to market opportunities, planted more soybeans. On the contrary, farmers in the south turned to another cash crop, cotton, which promised greater profits than soybeans, as I discuss below.

One food crop that did not follow the general trend was potatoes, the production of which rose substantially beginning in the 1910s. The center of potato production was in the eastern part of northern Korea. Compared with other crops, potatoes were highly productive per unit area, serving as an important food crop for poor farmers.

Finally, maize production also increased in the 1930s, mainly in the western part of northern Korea. One reason for this, which I discuss in more detail later, is that a large modern cornstarch factory using maize as a raw material was built in Pyongyang, thereby raising demand for maize.

Dissemination of Upland Cotton and Growth of Sericulture

Cotton was first cultivated as a summer crop on the Korean Peninsula in the fourteenth and fifteenth centuries, prior to its introduction to Japan. Cotton cultivation expanded during the Edo period in Japan, but it quickly declined after the Meiji Restoration in the face of cheap imports.

The Japanese government formulated policies designed to bolster, if only by a little, the production of raw cotton in regions under its control for use in the rapidly growing cotton textile industry at home.

In 1905, the Menka Saibai Kyokai (Cotton Cultivation Association) was founded in Tokyo, which established a seed orchard for upland cotton and a ginning mill in Korea. Upland cotton, which originated in South America and later improved upon in the United States, accounted for most of the raw cotton being cultivated globally at the time. The value of yarn spun from upland cotton was higher than that of yarn made from native Korean cotton.

After annexation, in 1911, the Government-General initiated its first six-year plan for the promotion of cotton production, which focused on replacing native cotton with upland cotton in southern Korea. The plan was extended one year and completed in 1918, at which time the area of land planted with upland cotton had increased to about 94,000 *chobu* (1 *chobu* = 0.992 hectares), close to the 100,000 *chobu* anticipated by the plan. During the same period, the area under native cotton cultivation declined from about 60,000 to about 36,000 *chobu*.

The second ten-year plan for the promotion of cotton production began in 1919. Major goals of this plan were to grow cotton by clearing new land for cultivation and converting existing fields to cotton and to increase yield per unit area by improving cultivation methods, with a focus on upland cotton in southern Korea and native cotton in the western part of northern Korea. In 1928, the final year of the plan, the cultivated area for upland and native cotton reached approximately 140,000 and 70,000 *chobu*, respectively.

During the period of plan implementation, however, the price of raw cotton declined, preventing the anticipated targets from being achieved. The price continued to decline after the term of the plan, prompting the Government-General to suspend further efforts to expand the cultivated area and concentrate instead on increasing production only through improvements in yield per unit area.

After the Manchurian Incident in 1931, a stable supply of raw cotton became even more important for the Japanese Empire. The Government-General accordingly formulated a new plan designed to increase both the amount of cultivated land devoted to cotton and the yield per unit area. In the 1930s, yield per unit area did not improve substantially, but the cultivation of upland cotton did expand, particularly in the western part of northern Korea.

Overall, upland cotton had a higher yield in terms of monetary value per unit area than native cotton. Its yield was even higher than that of the competing crop of soybeans, with some exceptional years. Upland cotton offered Korean farmers the long-term prospect of higher income, which explains why they converted their fields from native cotton and soybeans to upland cotton. Thus, the development of the Korean cotton crop under Japanese rule resulted in more than a six-fold increase in total production by the end of the 1930s as compared with the early 1910s.

Agricultural statistics for Korea show large increases in cultivated area and production amounts for many crops in the 1910s. It is difficult, however, to judge whether these increases actually occurred or whether, in those early years, insufficient surveys created apparent gains. Two crops that showed relatively high production values were *daikon* (white radish) and *hakusai* (Chinese cabbage). In both cases, however, production leveled off from the 1920s on.

Sericulture grew steadily throughout the period of Japanese rule. After annexation, the Government-General promoted sericulture by distributing improved breeds of silkworm and promoting mulberry cultivation and silkworm breeding techniques. In 1925, it formulated a fifteen-year plan to increase cocoon production by 1 million *koku*. Under a series of policies, there was a substantial increase in the number of cocooneries, the area of mulberry orchards, and the total output of cocoons. Farmers were engaged in sericulture as a rare side business to earn cash income.

2. Mining and Manufacturing: A Sudden Rise from an Undeveloped State

Growth Rates and the Policies of the Government-General

From 1911 to 1940, Korean mining and manufacturing industries grew sharply. In terms of real value added, the annual growth rate averaged about 12 percent for mining and 9 percent for manufacturing. Expansion was especially rapid in the 1930s, with annual growth rates approaching 20 percent and 10 percent, respectively.

It is generally said that the Government-General adopted suppressive policies toward the manufacturing industry in Korea in the 1910s, passive ones in the 1920s, and active ones in the 1930s. It is certainly true that, compared with the agricultural sector, the Government-General did not have much interest in industrialization in Korea in the 1910s and 1920s.

However, it cannot be said that the 1910s were an era of suppression. Many researchers mention the Company Ordinance as the main basis for suppressive policies. Promulgated by the Government-General in 1910, it required official permission for a company to be established. According to the "suppressionists," the purpose of this Ordinance was to prevent the development of commerce and industry in Korea, particularly Korean-owned capital. They stress that many applications to establish companies submitted by Koreans were rejected, but this view is simply the result of misreading the data. In fact, a high percentage of applications for company formation submitted by Koreans were approved.

Rice-Husking and -Polishing Plants Distinctive to Korea

Small and medium-sized businesses typically start up not as fully formed companies but instead under individual management. The first businesses to form in this manner in Korea were rice-husking and -polishing plants.

Traditionally, Korean rice farmers did not husk their own rice. They either sold their unhusked rice to huskers or polished their rice directly from the unhusked state (producing half-polished rice known as *kanpaku*, "Korean white") and sold it. After husking, the huskers either sold the unpolished brown rice to polishers or polished the rice themselves.

The husking and polishing industry in Korea rose before annexation when Japanese nationals established small-scale plants in rice distribution areas and at ports. Unhusked rice was more expensive to transport, and the moisture level of the half-polished rice made it prone to rot. This increased the importance of husking and polishing the rice before export, and the Japanese rice traders took this task upon themselves.

Koreans emulated the Japanese and began to enter the field. In 1912, there were 67 husking/polishing plants (with either 10 or more employees or motorized operations) run by Japanese nationals and 23 run by Koreans in all of Korea. Japanese-owned plants had an average of 30 employees, and Korean-owned plants had an average of 11. The plants were mostly small-scale operations, but there were some Japanese-owned plants that employed more than 200 workers.

In Japan, the usual practice was for farmers to husk their harvested rice using their own equipment and sell the resulting brown rice to retailers. The retailers polished the rice and sold it to consumers. Thus, Japan and Korea were different in this regard. The Korean practice of husking and polishing rice in factories was distinctive and contributed to reduced processing costs and more uniform quality of the product, which increased the market value of Korean rice. However, because Korean farmers entrusted husking operations to independent plants, they were forced to accept lower prices for the rice they harvested.

Husking and polishing operations grew in tandem with increased rice production and export. In 1932, there were 1,156 husking/polishing plants operating in Korea that employed five or more workers: 373 of them were operated by Japanese nationals and 783 by Koreans. Although the average size of the Korean-owned plants was smaller than that of the Japanese-owned plants, their total number was larger. Among Japanese-owned plants, some large plants emerged with a rice-polishing capacity exceeding 1 million *koku* per year. The largest of these was Chosen Seimai Kabushiki Kaisha (Korea Rice Polishing Company) operated by Kato Heitaro, a native of Yamaguchi Prefecture who was born in 1881 and was called the "king of rice polishing in Korea." By 1935, more than 30,000 workers were employed in rice-husking and -polishing plants in Korea.

Large-Scale Coal Development
Anthracite

In 1907, the Residency-General of Korea established Heijo Kogyosho, a mining office in Pyongyang, for the purpose of developing anthracite. After annexation, the Government-General took over operation of the enterprise and installed more equipment for coal extraction. Because most anthracite in Pyongyang took the form of coal dust, much of it was transported after extraction to the Briquette Manufactory of the Japanese Navy in Tokuyama, where it was processed into briquettes.

In 1922, management of Heijo Kogyosho was transferred from the Government-General to the Imperial Japanese Navy in response to the latter's request to emphasize the mining of Pyongyang anthracite. When the transfer was made, the Navy renamed Heijo Kogyosho as the Pyongyang Mining Division of the Naval Fuel Arsenal. In the 1920s, the Navy relocated some of the briquette manufacturing equipment from Tokuyama to Pyongyang, thus increasing the production capacity in the latter.

In 1928, the Pyongyang Mining Division achieved a coal output capacity of 140,000 tons per year, the highest output of any coal mining operation in Korea. In the same year, the Division manufactured 45,000 tons of briquettes, representing nearly half of all briquette production in Korea. During this period, nearly all of the briquettes were consumed in Korea to heat homes and power railway boilers.

In 1936, administrative reforms resulted in yet another change in the name of the mining office to the Mining Division of the Naval Fuel Arsenal. At the time, anthracite reserves in Pyongyang were estimated at between 500 and 600 million tons, an amount considered to be virtually limitless. The ancient capital of Pyongyang and coal production were historically linked; in fact, the city was nicknamed the "Coal Capital" because of its location over a vast coal field.

In the private sector, Chosen Muentan Kabushiki Kaisha (Korea Anthracite Company) was founded in 1927, in which Mitsubishi Seitetsu (Mitsubishi Iron and Steel Company) was the main investor. The company always maintained close ties with the Government-General as it mined anthracite in and around Pyongyang and manufactured briquettes.

Some of the highest quality anthracite in Korea was found at Ryuto Kogyosho (a mining operation in Yongdeung) in Pyeonganbuk-do in the northwestern part of northern Korea. This mine was developed by Katakura Shokusan (Katakura Industrial), which was affiliated with Katakura Seishi Boseki (Katakura Silk Reeling and Weaving Company). The unlikely connection between silk and coal can be explained by the suitability of anthracite as a means of heating cocooneries. Thus, anthracite contributed to the development of Korean sericulture. In 1935, Ryuto Kogyosho was producing about 60,000 tons of coal per year.

Anthracite was mined in southern Korea as well. Two mines in particular, located in the eastern part of southern Korea (the southern part of Gangwon-do), were well-known producers: the Samcheok coal mine and the Yeongwol coal mine. The former was operated by Sanchoku Kaihatsu (Sanchoku Development), a subsidiary of Nichiden Kogyo (a power company in Japan) established in 1936; the latter was operated by Chosen Denryoku (Korea Electric Power Company), a member of the Toyo Takushoku group. Coal reserves at the Samcheok coal mine were said to be enormous, totaling several hundred million tons. It was also the only mine in Korea that produced anthracite in non-dust form. For this reason, the coal from the Samcheok coal mine was mainly used in the production of carbide and castings.

Soft (Smoky) Coal
Most soft coal in Korea was low-grade (low-carbonization) lignite, not

the kind of high-quality coking coal found in Hokkaido and Kyushu in Japan. The soft coal produced in Korea was primarily used to power locomotives, but some was also sold for home heating. Compared with Japanese coal, Korean coal had a high chemical content that resulted in high reactivity with hydrogen. Therefore, it drew attention in the 1930s as a raw material for manufacturing synthetic oil (liquid fuel made by crushing coal and adding hydrogen). Production of soft coal in Korea was almost entirely limited to the north. Its development was undertaken by several big companies and sole proprietorships, including Meiji Kogyo (Meiji Mining) and Chosen Yuentan Kabushiki Kaisha (Korea Soft Coal Company).

Meiji Kogyo began developing coal and gold mines in Korea around the time of annexation. It obtained mining rights in Anju, Pyeongnam-do (in the southwestern part of northern Korea) and started operating a coal mine there in 1912, with reserves estimated at 50 million tons. The Anju coal mine was the first in Korea to be mechanized, with electric drills and drainage pumps manufactured by the German company Siemens in 1928. It produced lignite for home and railway applications. Another successful mine operated by Meiji Kogyo was the Sariwon coal mine, which was also located in the southwestern part of northern Korea, in Hwanghae-do. The company obtained mining rights in 1914 and opened the mine in 1931. The coal produced there was of nearly the same quality as coking coal, featuring good combustibility, strong thermal power, and clean burning, all of which made it suitable for use in furnaces and boilers.

Chosen Yuentan Kabushiki Kaisha was established in 1939, when small and medium-sized soft coal mines formed a consortium capitalized at 15 million yen through mediation efforts by the Government-General aimed at increasing coal production in Korea. The participating companies were Hokusen Tanko, Toyo Takushoku, Totaku Kogyo, and Aso Kosan, all of which contributed their mines as in-kind investments. Operations centered on the Gogeonwon coal mine in Hamgyeongbuk-do in the northeast. This mine, along with the Sariwon coal mine and the

Yuseon coal mine, was one of the main soft coal mines in Korea. In 1935, it had 3,000 employees and produced 30,000 tons of lignite annually. The quality of the coal was high, with a high calorific value (6,000 to 7,000 calories per gram) and low ash and sulfur content, making it a popular choice for railway and home heating use.

Among sole proprietorships, Iwamura Kogyo was particularly successful. It was founded by Iwamura Choichi, a native of Kumamoto Prefecture (1881–1948) who resided in Korea. In 1938, Yamaichi Shoken (Yamaichi Securities) bought a 40 percent stake to create a stock company capitalized at 10 million yen. Iwamura Kogyo operated several mines in northern Korea, including the Yuseon mine in Hamgyeongbuk-do. The Yuseon mine was one of the best in Korea in terms of both quality and quantity of the coal, which was sold for use in home heating and railway (express locomotives) applications.

Early Development of Iron Mines and Establishment of Ironworks
Dating to the 1910s, iron mine development got an early start in Korea and formed the basis for the construction of several ironworks. Immediately after annexation, the company Mitsubishi Goshi Kaisha (Mitsubishi Joint Company) purchased an iron mine in Gyeomipo, Pyeongannam-do (near the Daedong River) in the southwestern part of northern Korea. It subsequently continued to purchase nearby iron mines as well as anthracite coal mines in the same province and planned the construction of an ironworks.

Terauchi Masatake, the Imperial Japanese Army general who served as the first governor-general of Korea, played a leading role in this process. Through the mining bureau of the Governor-General, Terauchi helped Mitsubishi conduct mine surveys and smoothed the way for the disposal of large tracts of land owned by the Imperial Japanese Army in Gyeomipo. He also encouraged development by leasing to the company 400,000 *tsubo* (1 *tsubo* = 3.3 m^2) of property that had been earmarked for railway use and by waiving tariffs on imported construction supplies.

The construction of the ironworks in Gyeomipo (Kenjiho Seitetsujo) began in 1914, but work was substantially delayed by the outbreak of World War I. The facility was finally completed in 1918, and two blast furnaces with an annual production capacity of 50,000 tons each were activated. In the previous year, Mitsubishi had established Mitsubishi Seitetsu (headquartered in Tokyo), which was capitalized at 30 million yen. The operation of Gyeomipo Ironworks was entrusted to Mitsubishi Seitetsu.

Gyeomipo Ironworks introduced the most advanced technologies available at the time, including byproduct recovery furnaces. In 1919, an open-hearth furnace and rolling equipment manufactured by Mitsubishi Shipyards in Nagasaki and Kobe were added to create a fully integrated production system, ranging from pig iron to finished steel. A major purpose of production of the steel material was to supply Mitsubishi Shipyards with steel plate and large-scale pieces of steel for naval vessels. In 1921, the facility began producing high tensile strength steel plate for naval applications. In the same year, it increased pig iron production to 83,000 tons, steel production to 51,000 tons, and steel material production to 30,000 tons.

Subsequently, an economic downturn and a reduction in Japanese Navy forces resulted in a considerable decline in the steel market. In response, the company suspended operations at the steelmaking division of Gyeomipo Ironworks until 1933. Even during that time, however, the production capacity of its pig iron division increased, reaching 150,000 tons in 1931. This level was more than that of Kamaishi Ironworks in Japan, and slightly more than 20 percent of the production capacity of the largest steelmaking facility in the Japanese Empire, Yawata Ironworks.

In 1934, Nippon Seitetsu (Japan Iron and Steel Company) was created when Mitsubishi Seitetsu joined a large consortium of steel companies. The operation of Gyeomipo Ironworks was entrusted to the new company at that time. Immediately after Nippon Seitetsu was formed, a plan was formulated to expand the production facilities of all the companies under the consortium's umbrella. The blast furnaces at Gyeomipo

Ironworks were renovated, with furnace No. 1 being removed and replaced by a newly constructed 120,000-ton furnace. A new coke oven and a byproduct plant were also constructed. In 1934–35, open-hearth furnaces Nos. 2 and 3 began operations.

In the eastern part of northern Korea, the Yiwon iron mine began operating in the mid-1910s for the purpose of supplying Yawata Ironworks with iron ore. The ore mined at Yiwon was of relatively high quality, with an average iron content of 50–55 percent, and reserves were estimated at several tens of millions of tons. In 1927, the planned extraction amount was 80,000 tons.

The Yiwon iron mine had large amounts of fine ore that could not be processed with a blast furnace. To utilize it, Nihon Koshuha Jukogyo (Japan High-Frequency Heavy Industries) was founded in 1935. The new company built a factory in Seongjin, not far from Yiwon, and began making steel (special steel in particular) from fine ore using its electrical furnace technology.

The Musan iron mine was said to be one of the largest iron mines not only in Korea but all of East Asia, with estimated reserves of 1.5 billion tons. Located deep in the northeastern part of northern Korea, it was hard to access and full development did not begin until the second half of the 1930s. In chapter 4, I discuss in detail how Nippon Seitetsu began construction of an ironworks in Cheongjin in 1939, which used ore from the Musan mine.

A Large-Scale Nonferrous Metal Refinery
During the rule of the Residency-General, Kuhara Kogyo (Kuhara Mining Company) began a geological survey of Korea. Kuhara Kogyo was the precursor of Nippon Kogyo, a leading mining company in Japan before World War II and one of the predecessors of JXTG Holdings, Inc. today.

Beginning in 1915, Kuhara Kogyo aggressively pursued the development of gold, silver, copper, lead, and zinc mines in northern Korea. It also planned the construction of a refinery to process gold, silver, and copper ore. The new plant was sited at Jinnampo (on the outskirts of Pyongyang), which was convenient for shipping by sea. Construction began in May 1915, and operations began in October of that year. Initially, the plant had a production capacity of 216 tons of crude copper per month and employed 1,400 workers.

Facilities at the refinery were subsequently expanded, including the completion of a 600-foot (183-meter) chimney in 1936, the tallest in the world at the time. In locations such as Ashio and Besshi in Japan, smoke from metal refineries had caused serious damage to forests and farms. The tall chimney was intended to prevent the same kinds of problems from occurring in and around Jinnampo.

The Forgotten Munitions Plant

There was a munitions plant in Pyongyang when Korea was under Japanese rule. After World War II, this fact was forgotten not only by the general public but also by most scholars of modern Korean history. Because the plant was under the direct control of the Imperial Japanese Army, no records of it were included in materials that would ordinarily be viewed by those scholars, particularly publications of the Government-General. *The Annual Administration Report of the Government-General of Korea* does not mention the plant, and industrial statistics announced by the Government-General do not include the outputs at the plant.

The munitions plant in Pyongyang, however, was not a secret facility. Located near the center of Pyongyang, it was familiar to city residents before WWII. Built in 1917, the plant was originally called the Korea Munitions Plant (Chosen Heiki Seizosho) and was attached to the Tokyo artillery arsenal. Subsequently, it underwent two transformations before becoming Pyongyang Munitions Plant (Heijo Heiki Seizosho) under the jurisdiction of the Kokura arsenal of the Japanese Army armory in 1936.

The main products of the plant included artillery shells, aircraft bombs, rolling stock, leather goods, weapons partially made of hemp, and materials for the manufacture of instruments. Nearly 200 workers were employed at the plant in 1923, but this number subsequently increased, reaching about 450 by 1936. In that year, armories in Japan employed thousands of people (one in Osaka had more than 8,000 workers). Compared with the plant in Osaka, the workforce at Pyongyang Munitions Plant was quite small. Also, compared with the standard size of ordinary factories in Japan, the plant was only of medium size. In the Korean context, however, it was considered to be a large factory.

The Growth of Onoda Cement

Immediately after annexation, a primary cement maker in Japan, Onoda Cement, set about establishing operations in Korea to meet anticipated growth in demand for cement for railway, road, harbor, and other construction projects. Limestone, an ingredient in cement, could be found in vast quantities in various regions of Korea, particularly in the north.

Completed in the suburbs of Pyongyang in 1919, the new Onoda Cement plant had cutting-edge equipment for the time, with an annual production capacity of 34,000 tons. Onoda Cement later expanded the plant at Pyongyang and built two more in the eastern part of northern Korea, one in Wonsan in 1928 and another in Gomusan in 1936.

In the second half of the 1920s, the combined supply capacity of the plants in Pyongyang and Wonsan exceeded total demand for cement in Korea. Onoda Cement therefore restricted production at these plants and set its sights on selling its products in Japan and Manchuria.

The competitors of Onoda Cement, Ube Cement and Asano Cement, countered Onoda's business strategy by constructing large plants in Korea in the second half of the 1930s (Ube in 1936 and Asano in 1937, both in the western part of northern Korea).

The Development of the Silk Industry and the Cotton-Spinning and Weaving Industry

Katakura Seishi Boseki was founded in 1920. Its predecessor, Katakura Gumi, made plans to enter the Korean market after the Sino-Japanese War and initiated a survey of Korean sericulture and silk industries. After annexation, Katakura Gumi established forestry divisions in several locations in northern Korea. In 1913, it opened a cocoon purchasing office in the southern Korean town of Daegu, and went on to build a silk-reeling factory there in 1918.

In 1919, the silk company Yamaju Gumi, which was based in Shinshu, Japan, also built a factory in Daegu. In the same year, Yamamoto Jotaro, who began his career at Mitsui Bussan (Mitsui & Co.) and later served as the president of the South Manchuria Railway Company, teamed up with Ozawa Gumi and other companies in Shinshu to establish Chosen Kiito Kabushiki Kaisha (Korea Raw Silk Company), which also set up operations in Daegu. Thus, Daegu became the center of mechanized silk reeling in Korea.

In 1927–28, Katakura Seishi Boseki established more factories in Seoul (the company purchased a small factory and expanded it), Ham-heung (in the eastern part of northern Korea), and Jeonju (in the western part of southern Korea). At about the same time, Gunze Seishi, Toyo Seishi, and Zenhoku Seishi (the latter two affiliated with Mitsui Bussan) also built factories in Korea.

Koreans also established silk-reeling companies and built factories. Two of the more prominent Korean-owned companies were Chosen Seishi and Chunan Seishi. The former was founded in 1919 by a no-bleman who belonged to the Korean aristocracy prior to the Japanese colonial period; its factory was located in Seoul. The latter was founded in 1926 with a factory located in the central part of southern Korea.

Many other small-scale factories were set up throughout Korea under both Japanese and Korean ownership and management. At the end of 1934, there were 84 mechanized silk-reeling factories operating in Korea with a workforce of five or more employees. Forty percent (34) of these were operated by Koreans, and 19 of those were located in Daegu.

In the area of cotton spinning and weaving, Chosen Boshoku Kabu-shiki Kaisha (Korea Spinning and Weaving Company) was established in 1917 by Noda Utaro (who participated in the founding of Miike Bo-seki), Magoshi Kyohei (who used to work at Mitsui Bussan), Yamamoto Jotaro, and others. The company set up operations in Busan and built a large spinning and weaving factory there in 1922.

In 1919, the Kim family, who had vast landholdings in the western part of southern Korea, established Keijo Boshoku Kabushiki Kaisha (Keijo Spinning and Weaving Company). The company bought and operated a small factory that previously belonged to Keijo Orihimo Kaisha, which was set up in 1910. The factory subsequently achieved remarkable growth. Keijo Boshoku also built cotton ginning plants and dyeing plants all over Korea and became one of the preeminent Korean-owned companies. Underlying this growth was generous financial support provided by Chosen Shokusan Ginko (Korea Industrial Bank), a half-public, half-private financial institution founded by the Government-General (Eckert 2004, 87–102). In the 1930s, two of Japan's major cotton-spinning and weaving companies, Toyobo and Kanebo, built factories in Korea.

One example of a Korean-initiated small to medium-sized business in the cotton-weaving field was a factory in Pyongyang that made knitted socks. It was founded by a Korean resident in Pyongyang in 1906, who introduced machinery from Japan. The sock-knitting industry grew sharply in the 1920s, and there were 33 cotton sock plants operating in Pyongyang by 1934. Nearly all of them were small plants that employed fewer than 50 workers, but three of them employed 100 to 200 workers.

Pulp and Paper Industry Led by Oji Seishi

Oji Seishi (Oji Pulp Company) became the driving force of the pulp and paper industry in Korea. The ample conifer forests on the banks of the Yalu River enticed Oji Seishi to set up operations in Korea at an early date. In 1917, the company founded a subsidiary called Chosen Seishi, which constructed a pulp mill in the following year in Sinuiju, located on the border between the northwestern part of northern Korea and Manchuria. The mill produced sulfite pulp and ground pulp from raw wood, and supplied its products to paper mills operated by Oji Seishi in Japan.

The Government-General supported Chosen Seishi and preferentially sold government-owned lumber grown and harvested in the Yalu

River basin to the company. The pulp mill in Sinuiju had a site area of 210,000 *tsubo* and an annual production capacity of 10,000 tons, making it one of the largest factories in Korea. After experiencing a downturn following World War I, the mill in Sinuiju was expanded in 1925 and began to produce rolled paper.

Furthermore, Oji Seishi undertook to develop virgin forest in Hamgyeong-do in the eastern part of northern Korea. In 1935, it established a subsidiary called Hokusen Seishi Kagaku Kogyo (Hokusen Paper and Chemical Industry), which constructed a mill in Gilju in the eastern part of northern Korea. This was the first mill in the world to produce rayon pulp (an intermediate material for chemical fiber) using larch wood as raw material. Gilju Mill had an annual production capacity of 25,000 tons, which was more than that of competitive pulp mills operating in Japan. In 1937, Gilju Mill accounted for 36 percent of all rayon pulp produced in the Japanese Empire. Rayon textiles were one of Japan's main export products at the time, and Gilju Mill served an important function as an intermediate material processor.

Noguchi Shitagau and the Development of Large-Scale Electric Power and Chemical Plants

After annexation, the Government-General actively conducted surveys on hydroelectric power sources in Korea. The first round of surveys was implemented from 1911 to 1914, the second from 1922 to 1929, and the third was initiated in 1936. Each round resulted in an expansion in the number of hydroelectric power sources amenable to development. Most of them were on the Yalu and Tumen rivers and their tributaries in northern Korea.

In 1926, Noguchi Shitagau (1873–1944) founded Chosen Suiryoku Hatsuden Kabushiki Kaisha (Korea Hydroelectric Power Company) with a capitalization of 20 million yen and began hydraulic development on the Bujeon River, a tributary of the Yalu River. Noguchi was originally an engineer from the electrical engineering department of Tokyo Imperial University, but became an entrepreneur in 1908 with the establishment of Nippon Chisso Hiryo Kabushiki Kaisha (Japan Nitrogen Fertilizer Company), which manufactured chemical fertilizer.

The Bujeon River flowed to the north of the Gaema Plateau and converged with the Yalu River. Noguchi planned to change its course through watershed modification to achieve large-scale power generation. The first step was to build a dam to flood valleys and create an artificial lake along the river. The next task was to dig water transmission tunnels through the mountains to drop water from the reservoir into the Sea of Japan. Noguchi's inventive idea was to utilize the difference in elevation between the reservoir and the ocean to generate electricity. He further planned to construct power plants in four locations. The huge scale of electric power development on the Bujeon River was unprecedented in the Japanese Empire. To initiate the project required the construction of a railroad for material transport. The first power plant was finally completed in 1929.

Using the same methodology, Noguchi was also engaged in the development of power sources on the Jangjin and Heocheon rivers, two other tributaries of the Yalu River. Construction of power plants on these rivers began in 1933 and 1937, respectively. The scale of both of these projects surpassed that of the Bujeon project.

Noguchi's ultimate goal was to build a chemical fertilizer plant in northern Korea that would have access to ample and inexpensive electrical power. He invested 10 million yen to establish Chosen Chisso Hiryo Kabushiki Kaisha (Korea Nitrogen Fertilizer Company) in 1927 (which merged with its parent company, Nippon Chisso Hiryo, in 1941), and began the construction of a plant in Heungnam (in the eastern part of northern Korea), which was completed in 1929.

The Heungnam Fertilizer Plant comprised facilities engaged in ammonia synthesis, electrolysis, ammonium sulfate manufacture, machinery manufacture, and catalysis. It had an initial production capacity of ammonium sulfate of 400,000 tons annually, which far exceeded that of Nippon Chisso Hiryo's plants in Japan (in Nobeoka and Minamata). Unlike the equipment in the plants in Japan, which had mostly been imported from Europe and North America, all of the equipment in the Heungnam Fertilizer Plant (except the nitrogen separator) had been manufactured by Japanese companies (including Yasukawa Denki, Fuji Denki, Shibaura Seisakusho, Kobe Seikosho, and Hitachi Seisakusho). Thus, the construction of this plant provided a strong stimulus for the development of the machinery industry in Japan.

Iron sulfide is essential for the manufacture of sulfuric acid, and these were procured from mines in Japan and throughout Korea. The main source in Japan was the Yanahara mine in Okayama Prefecture; in Korea in the 1930s, Iron sulfide was mainly mined in the northeast. To promote the development of Iron sulfide mines in Korea, Noguchi invested 1 million yen to establish Chosen Kogyo Kaihatsu Kabushiki Kaisha (Korea Mining Development Company) in 1929.

After its founding, the Heungnam Fertilizer Plant continued to expand. In addition to ammonium sulfate, its output was diversified to include ammonium sulfate-phosphate, superphosphate of lime, lime nitrogen, and other products, which it shipped in large quantities within Korea and to Japan.

A World-Class Chemical Industrial Complex

Noguchi constructed another chemical plant, in Bongung, about four kilometers from the Heungnam Fertilizer Plant. It began processing soybeans in 1936. Construction was completed on a lime nitrogen facility in July of that year, enabling the mass manufacture of caustic soda (sodium hydroxide), ammonium chloride, carbide, lime nitrogen, and other products. The manufacturing method for caustic soda was perfected at the Nobeoka plant in Japan and involved the electrolysis of salt using the mercury process. The caustic soda was then shipped to affiliated chemical plants.

The manufacturing of ammonium chloride was initiated with the intention of making effective use of the chlorine that was produced through the electrolysis of salt. In Korea, ammonium chloride was either sold as fertilizer or purified and sold to manufacturers of batteries.

Chlorine was also used as a raw material in the manufacturing of hydrochloric acid, bleaching powder, and liquid chlorine. It was rare even in Japan for a single plant to manufacture multiple chemical products simultaneously through the rationalized use of salt.

Limestone, a raw material used to make carbide, was transported by freight cars to the plant from a limestone quarry owned by the company and located north of Bongung. When there was a shortage, the rest was procured from the Onoda Cement plant in Wonsan.

At the chemical plant in Bongung, large amounts of powdered carbide generated as a byproduct of the carbide manufacturing process were simply thrown away. To avoid such waste, technology was developed that enabled the utilization of powdered carbide, which provided the basis for the construction of branch facilities dedicated to the production of acetylene, acetylene black, and glycol. Acetylene black was sold primarily as a material for making printing ink and rubber filler. At the glycol facility, hydrogen was added to acetylene to produce ethylene, the base material for manufacturing glycol. Other products made from acetylene included butanol and acetone. Glycol, butanol, and acetone are basic chemical products used to make solvents, synthetic resins, pharmaceuticals, and other products.

Noguchi built one related factory after another to create a huge chemical industrial complex in Heungnam, one of the largest in the world. Meanwhile Noguchi also pursued urban development in Heungnam, including the construction of a harbor and housing. This was a unique feature of industrial development in Heungnam: a private-sector entrepreneur was engaged in development of infrastructure and factory construction at the same time.

Noguchi's Other Projects

Noguchi's projects extended beyond Heungnam. In 1932, he built a coal carbonization plant in the town of Yeongan in Hamgyeongbuk-do in the northeastern part of northern Korea. Using lignite available nearby, the plant manufactured gasoline from tar and produced methanol and formalin from water gas. Formalin is a base material used to make explosives and carbolic resin (Bakelite). The plant in Yeongan included chemical facilities, machinery manufacturing facilities, and an in-house thermal power plant. The power plant burned semicoke and supplied power not just to the plant but also to surrounding cities through an electric power company (Chosen Denki).

In 1935, on the basis of technological development in Yeongan, Noguchi founded Chosen Sekitan Kogyo Kabushiki Kaisha (Korea Coal Industry Company), a new firm that was capitalized at 10 million yen and engaged in direct coal liquefaction. While operating the plant in Yeongan, the company built another plant in Aoji in 1936, in the extreme northeastern corner of northern Korea, near the borders of Manchuria and the Soviet Union. The plant in Aoji featured cutting-edge equipment such as high-efficiency gas generators and Japan's first 5,000-hp gas compressors, which were capable of generating 240 atmospheres of pressure each. All of the important equipment at the plant was manufactured by Japanese companies, including Kobe Seikosho and Hitachi Seisakusho, and the Kure Naval Arsenal. For raw material, it used lignite obtained from a nearby company-owned mine. Technological development was avidly pursued by engineers from the naval fuel arsenal in Tokuyama. They were joined by Professor Oshima Yoshikiyo of Tokyo Imperial University, an authority on fuel science. At its peak, the plant had a production capacity of 50,000 tons of liquefied coal per year.

Research and commercialization of liquid fuel made from coal had already been undertaken by the Germans, British, and Americans. In Japan, the Navy first showed an interest, with the Japanese government formulating its "Summary Plan for the Promotion of Artificial Petroleum" in 1936 and implementing the "national liquid fuel policy" in the following year. In this context, Noguchi pursued the commercialization of liquefied coal in Korea.

Noguchi gathered many talented engineers and guided them as they introduced and developed advanced technologies. Funding was initially provided by Mitsubishi Ginko (Mitsubishi Bank), with financing later provided by Nippon Kogyo Ginko (The Industrial Bank of Japan) and two of Korea's main financial institutions: Chosen Ginko and Chosen Shokusan Ginko. Noguchi had close connections with the Government-General and was particularly close to Ugaki Kazushige, the sixth governor-general. Ugaki had a strong interest in Noguchi's enterprises and assisted in their development.

The Overlooked Machine Industry

It is widely said that the machine industry languished in Korea under Japanese rule, but this is not true. It did grow during the colonial period, although not as flamboyantly as the other sectors, particularly the chemical industry.

Many of the Japanese companies that built metal and chemical plants in Korea added machinery manufacturing facilities where they produced and repaired the machinery used in their plants. Because these machine shops did not take the form of independent companies or factories, they hardly ever appear in the statistics and data of the time. Nevertheless, they still played an important role in Korean industrialization.

The machine plant in Heungnam was the largest machine manufacturing facility in Korea. It was constructed in 1928, at the same time that the Heungnam Fertilizer Plant was built. It expanded as the chemical industrial complex in Heungnam developed, and manufactured, renovated, and repaired the machinery needed by the industrial complex. Nearly all of the newly designed machines were manufactured at this plant. It possessed a full complement of equipment comparable to that of an independent machine manufacturing company, including electric furnaces for casting, large hammers for forging, various lathes, and presses for manufacturing cans.

The Railway Bureau of the Government-General also operated machine manufacturing facilities throughout Korea. The largest of these was the plant in Seoul, founded in 1905. This plant started out as a small railway repair facility but gradually expanded. In 1927, it started producing steam locomotives. By 1939, it had 854 machine tools and a workforce of 1,700 skilled men (of which 595 were Japanese).

Two powerful independent machine manufacturing companies should also be mentioned: Chosen Shoko and Ryuzan Kosaku. Chosen Shoko Kabushiki Kaisha (Korea Industrial and Commerce Company) was established in 1919 by Nakamura Seishichiro, a Japanese national living in Korea. Born in 1872 in Nagasaki Prefecture, Nakamura founded Nakamura Gumi, a sea transport company. Active in many commercial and industrial fields, including civil engineering, oil, fertilizer, machinery, ironworking, shipbuilding, and transport, Chosen Shoko was known as the "Mitsui Bussan of the Peninsula" and was the predecessor of Sankyu, Inc., a modern-day general distribution company based in Kyushu. Its first plant was built in Jinnampo in 1910, and it engaged in the manufacture and repair of mining and refining machinery. The origin of Ryuzan Kosaku Kabushiki Kaisha (Ryuzan Manufacturing Company) was an ironworks founded in 1919 by Tagawa Tsunejiro, a native of Shimane Prefecture who was born in 1884. Affiliated with the Railway Bureau, it grew quite large by the 1930s, operating plants that manufactured locomotives, rolling stock for passenger and freight trains, and various other railway equipment in Seoul and Incheon.

Rubber Processing, Fish Oil Manufacture, and Agricultural Product Processing

Rubber processing plants (mainly for rubber boots) flourished in Pyongyang starting in the 1920s. Nearly all of them were small-scale enterprises owned by Koreans, although several of them developed workforces of 100 people or more. In 1939, there were 13 rubber processing plants in Pyongyang, only one of which was Japanese-owned. Two of them had workforces in excess of 200 people.

The fish oil business prospered with the growth of the sardine fishing industry. In 1923, large schools of migrating sardines suddenly appeared off the eastern coast of Korea. In response, Japanese nationals introduced Japanese-style purse seine fishing using motorized boats, giving birth to a burgeoning sardine fishing industry. In the first half of the

1930s, Japanese companies founded modern fish processing plants near fishing harbors, including Chosen Chisso's oil plant in Heungnam and a Chosen Yushi (Korea Oil and Fat Company) plant in Cheongjin. These plants produced large volumes of sardine oil (used in the manufacturing of soap, foodstuffs, and pharmaceuticals) and fish meal (for fertilizer). Meanwhile, many Korean-owned small-scale plants for fish-oil processing sprang up, numbering more than a thousand by the late 1930s. At that time, Korean sardine oil accounted for three-quarters of all sardine oil produced in the Japanese Empire and was an important resource for the oil industry both in Japan and Korea. Reaching its peak in about 1940, the Korean sardine fishing industry was on a global scale. (Subsequently, the sardines stopped migrating near Korea and the industry rapidly declined, bringing an end to fish-oil processing in this area.)

A noteworthy development in the field of agricultural product processing in Korea occurred in 1931, when Nippon Corn Products built a corn processing plant in Pyongyang. The company was a subsidiary of an American company (with some investment by Mitsubishi). Introducing American-style machine technology, it processed maize grown in Korea and Manchuria to make such products as cornstarch and dextrose. The cornstarch was important both as food (mixed with rice and barley) and for industrial applications, including newly developed ones such as pigment and gunpowder manufacture. The plant in Pyongyang became the largest of its kind in Asia.

An Overview:
Mining Output, Total Number of Plants, and Proportion of Heavy and Chemical Industries

From annexation in 1910 to 1935, coal production increased drastically from 80,000 to 2 million tons per year (table 2-2). Iron ore increased from 140,000 tons to 230,000 tons. Production of graphite (used to make desiccants, steelmaking crucibles, and electrodes), barite (the source ore of barium sulfate, a chemical additive), tungsten (for making metal alloys), and various other minerals also increased. The district of Ganggye in Pyeonganbuk-do in the northwestern part of northern Korea was known worldwide as a source of vein graphite. Other products that do not appear in table 2-2 include rare minerals such as antimony and mica, which were mined in the 1920s. In the 1930s, extraction began at a magnesite mine in Dancheon in Hamgyeongnam-do in the eastern part of northern Korea. It had one of the largest magnesite reserves in the world, estimated at several hundred million tons of high-grade ore.

The total number of industrial plants in Korea increased approximately from 300 to 6,500 between 1912 and 1939 (table 2-3). This increase was particularly evident among Korean-owned plants, which first surpassed the number of Japanese-owned plants in 1932. Although most Korean-owned plants were quite modest in size, with fewer than

Table 2-2.

Ore Production in Korea, 1910–35

(1,000 tons)

	Gold and silver	Copper	Zinc	Iron (pig iron)	Iron sulfide	Graphite	Coal	Barite	Fluorite	Tungsten	Quartz	Alunite
1910	10.3	0.4	—	140.4 (—)	—	0.8	78.5	—	—	—	—	—
1915	8.8	0.0	8.1	259.2 (—)	—	0.5	229.1	—	—	—	—	—
1920	21.5	—	3.4	447.2 (85.2)	—	11.2	289.0	—	—	—	28.8	—
1925	17.0	1.0	3.5	351.4 (101.9)	—	14.1	622.3	—	—	—	75.9	—
1930	13.4	5.6	3.8	532.5 (151.4)	—	20.1	884.1	6.1	2.3	0.0	47.3	11.7
1935	58.1	1.6	2.2	228.2 (147.8)	55.6	45.1	1,991.2	11.0	9.7	0.9	38.7	81.5

Sources: The Government-General of Korea 1933, *Chosen Sotokufu tokei nempo: Showa 6 nen*, 182–185; and The Government-General of Korea 1937, *Chosen Sotokufu tokei nempo: Showa 10 nen*, 149–151.

Table 2-3.

Number of Plants by Size and Ownership in Korea, 1912–39

Employees (no. of factory workers)	1912		1932		1939	
	Japanese-owned	Korean-owned	Japanese-owned	Korean-owned	Japanese-owned	Korean-owned
5-49	159 (77.9)	87 (92.6)	1,887 (92.5)	2,445 (97.7)	2,040 (80.1)	3,731 (95.2)
50-99	27 (13.2)	3 (3.2)	82 (4.0)	40 (1.6)	231 (9.1)	135 (3.4)
100-199	11 (5.4)	2 (2.1)	33 (1.6)	12 (0.5)	150 (5.9)	38 (1.0)
200+	7 (3.4)	2 (2.1)	39 (1.6)	5 (0.2)	125 (4.9)	15 (0.4)
Total	204 (100)	94 (100)	2,041 (100)	2,502 (100)	2,546 (100)	3,919 (100)

Note: Figures for 1912 indicate plants that employed ten or more people or that utilized motors. Figures for 1932 and 1939 indicate plants with facilities that employed five or more factory workers or plants that employed five or more factory workers at all times. Figures in parentheses indicate the percentage of the total number of plants accounted for by plants of the indicated size.
Source: Umemura and Mizoguchi 1988, 52.

50 employees, some relatively large plants also developed, with 15 plants employing 200 or more workers by 1939. Many Japanese-owned plants were also small and medium-sized, but their average size was larger than that of their Korean-owned counterparts. Japanese-owned plants accounted for 90 percent of all large-scale plants, far outnumbering those owned by Koreans.

Not only did industry as a whole experience growth, but the proportion of total industrial output accounted for by heavy and chemical industries (machinery, metals, and chemicals) increased from only 6 percent in 1911 to 12 percent in 1920, 17 percent in 1930, and 40 percent in 1939.

3. Participation of Koreans
in the Remarkable Development

Transition to a Non-Agricultural Economy

Under Japanese rule, the Korean economy underwent momentous changes, so much so that, from a global perspective, it constituted an exceptional case in the first half of the twentieth century. In short, it represented a rapid transition from a primarily agricultural economy to a primarily non-agricultural one. During this transition, the agricultural sector itself underwent change. The policies of the Government-General and the development of the money economy led to improved farming techniques and changes in crop selection. Overall agricultural production increased steadily. Industrialization in Korea began with small and medium-sized plants that simply processed raw materials. Then, as early as the 1910s, modern industries arose, particularly ironmaking plants. From the 1920s until the 1930s, a private enterprise built a large-scale chemical industrial complex founded on the development of power plants. The Government-General pushed construction of infrastructure such as transportation and communications networks and simultaneously supported industrial development in several sectors from the earliest days after annexation. The scope of those activities was expanded in the late 1920s and thereafter.

From the perspective of comparative economic history, the industrialization observed in Korea during this period never occurred in Western colonies. This contrast between Japanese rule over Korea and Western colonization is particularly evident with regard to the construction of hydroelectric power plants on a scale beyond those in the home country (Japan in this case), as well as the giant industrial complex that relied on them. What must be emphasized here is that the colonized people themselves contributed widely to industrialization in Korea. It is true that the Government-General and Japanese nationals (both companies and individuals) led the way and official policy coupled with Japanese financing, technology, and know-how played central roles. But at the same time, Koreans positively responded to external stimulus and took the initiative in following Japanese models and learning skills in business and industrial technologies, thereby demonstrating their own entrepreneurship. The remarkable development achieved was thus the result of the combined efforts of the colonizer and the colonized.

From this point of view, the shortcomings of the so-called "colonial dependence theory" become apparent. On the basis of Marxian economics, the dependence theory has had a strong impact on researchers and other intellectuals interested in colonial history. It focuses attention on the relationships of dominance/subordination and exploiter/exploited that play out between a colonizing country and its colony. Such a view reduces the colonized to a group of totally powerless people, ignoring the positive contributions they make to economic growth. Today, Marxism is in decline, but the emotionally charged issues of inflicting/suffering harm and atonement have gained currency, and the deeply rooted dependence theory has been maintained. This perspective, however, cannot ultimately explain the changes in the Korean economy from the 1910s through the 1930s.

The Small Presence of Chinese
Finally, the small presence of Chinese nationals in Korea during this period merits consideration. Chinese nationals (ethnic Chinese born in Qing China or the Republic of China) made up less than 0.5 percent of the total population in colonial Korea. This distinguishes Korea from the colonies in Southeast Asia, all of which had a relatively large Chinese presence.

In Southeast Asia, the western colonizers lived in limited districts, especially urban locations, and tended to work either in administration and international trade or on plantations. In these countries, most Chinese worked as laborers in agriculture or civil engineering projects, or in small to medium enterprises operating in such fields as commerce, transportation, and food processing (e.g., rice polishing), or in marginal administrative positions. In these capacities, the Chinese supplemented the economic activity and reign of the Western colonizers. Thus, new economic opportunities were monopolized by the hard-working and adaptive Chinese, and as a result, the colonized population was unable to free itself from work centered on traditional agriculture (Myint 1971, 80–82).

This phenomenon did not occur in Korea, where the economic activity of Chinese nationals was limited to such small areas as vegetable farming and China-related trade. Had there been a larger Chinese population in Korea, it would probably have been much more difficult for Koreans to participate in new business ventures. Indeed, they may well have been placed below the Chinese in the economic pecking order. The lack of Chinese influence, then, should not be dismissed, as has been done in the past, on the issue of the industrialization of Korea under Japanese rule.

Column 1.

Japanese Engineers Working in Korea

Chosen gijutsusha meibo (List of Engineers in Korea) was published in 1939. It is a book listing engineers of Japanese and Korean origin who lived in Korea at that time. It contained the names of elite engineers who graduated from universities or colleges, the university/college they graduated from, the subjects they majored in, and their place of work.

According to the book, there were about 6,700 engineers in Korea, 5,700 of which were of Japanese origin and the rest were Korean. This is noteworthy because so many engineers went to Korea from Japan and the engineers of Korean origin were educated and trained when Korea was under Japanese rule.

Japanese engineers who majored in agriculture formed the largest group (over 1,100), followed by those who majored in civil engineering, forestry, chemistry, and mining. In terms of their place of work, about 2,500 worked for central and local government offices, followed by about 2,000 for private companies. (Others worked for the military, academic institutions, and other miscellaneous organizations.) These data indirectly indicate that the Government-General was not a mere governing organization, but it also was an institution that was involved in the development of agricultural and civil engineering.

Among the private companies, the largest number of Japanese engineers (217) worked for companies related to Noguchi Shitagau (the Nicchitsu zaibatsu conglomerate). In particular, applied chemical engineers that had graduated from Tokyo Imperial University were concentrated at companies related to Noguchi. At that time, they possessed the highest level of knowledge in their field, enough to teach university students.

One such elite engineer was Munakata Eiji (1908–2004) who completed the course at the Applied Chemical Department, Faculty of Engineering at Tokyo Imperial University, and landed a job at Japan Bemberg

Fiber Co., Ltd. in 1931, with a recommendation from Professor Oshima Yoshikiyo. Japan Bemberg Fiber (present-day Asahi Kasei Corporation) was established in Nobeoka by Noguchi. Munakata was involved in the research and development of manufacturing artificial silk and was awarded a patent for his unique invention of an ammonia recovery method. In 1939, Noguchi transferred Munakata to take on an assignment at Chosen Sekitan Kogyo Kabushiki Kaisha (Korea Coal Industry Company). Munakata went to Korea and worked at the plant in Aoji to promote a coal liquification project. In 1944, he moved to Heungnam, where he worked to develop a technology for extracting alumina, the raw material used for producing aluminum, out of clay (Jangsan clay) produced in northern Korea. During this period, he also taught chemical engineering at the Faculty of Science and Engineering at Keijo Imperial University (established in 1924 as the only university in Korea).

Munakata learned of the end of World War II in Heungnam. Occupation forces from the Soviet Union stationed in northern Korea did not allow Japanese engineers to return to Japan and forced them to operate the factories. Munakata was among them and worked as a technical instructor at Heungnam People's Plant (formerly Heungnam Fertilizer Plant) to help revitalize its production capacity. He escaped from northern Korea by sea and returned to Japan by way of South Korea at the end of 1946.

Munakata became director of Asahi Kasei Corporation after his return to Japan and contributed to the rehabilitation of the artificial silk industry. He was appointed as director of the Japan Atomic Energy Research Institute in 1962 (and then its director-general from 1968 to 1978).

CHAPTER
3

Standards of Living

As mentioned in the Preface, it is taken for granted that the Korean people were impoverished under Japanese rule and their standard of living declined. But what empirical foundation does this assertion have?

The concept of "standard of living" is complex and contains subjective elements; it should not be discussed in simplistic terms. In this chapter, I explore this issue, taking the results of recent research into consideration.

1. The Fall of Farmers

The Adverse Effect of Introducing a Money Economy

Economic growth in underdeveloped regions does not necessarily result in the improvement of living standards among the general population. In fact, it can lead to a decline in general living standards in the short term, as a byproduct of the introduction of a money economy into traditional rural society. Farmers who have long lived in a "subsistence economy" are not be adept at organizing cash management for their households. Lured by new manufactured products, they can easily overspend. They also have little understanding of market mechanisms and lack the ability to adapt to changes in the price of cash crops. As a result, some farmers fall into heavy debt, lose their land, and are reduced to tenant farming (Myint 1965, 48).

Did this happen in Korea? According to statistics on farm households, the total number of owner-cultivators (self-sufficient land-owning farmers) and owner-tenants (land-owning farmers who must rent additional land to cultivate for income) fell from 1.5 million to 1.3 million between 1918 and 1940. Conversely, the number of pure tenants (farmers who rent the whole land they cultivate) rose from 1 million to 1.6 million during the same period. Many scholars interpret this to mean that Korean farmers became impoverished, but the data show that the increment of pure tenants (600,000 households) far exceeded the decrement of owner-cultivators and owner-tenants (200,000 households). It is certainly true that, as observers at the time indicated, some farm owners were reduced to tenant status. But this alone does not explain the increase in pure tenant farmers. Looking at the area of cultivated land during the period in question, there was about a 12 percent reduction in the area cultivated by owner farmers and a nearly 20 percent increase in the area cultivated by tenant farmers. This means that there was a significant increase in tenant farming due to the clearing of new land. To find out if the Korean farming population did indeed become impoverished, we must analyze a broad range of related materials.

2. Personal Consumption: Did the Consumption of Food Drastically Decline?

Per Capita Food Consumption

Rice consumption has received a great deal of attention. As I discussed in the previous chapter, the production of rice increased greatly under Japanese rule. However, because much of that rice was exported to Japan, it is said that the per capita consumption of rice in Korea greatly declined. This phenomenon was pointed out in 1935 by the two famous agricultural economists Tohata Seiichi and Ohkawa Kazushi in their book, *Chosen beikoku keizai ron* (Rice Economy in Korea). They assert that per capita annual rice consumption in Korea averaged 0.7071 *koku* in 1915–19, but that it declined considerably thereafter, down to 0.4486 *koku* by 1930–33. Tohata and Ohkawa also note that consumption of millet, which should have supplemented rice consumption, barely increased during the same period, calling it the "dark side of consumer life among Korean farmers" (Tohata and Ohkawa 1935, 86–93).

Until recently, the conclusions reached by Tohata and Ohkawa based on their calculations (or similar statistics) were repeatedly quoted and widely known among people interested in modern Korean history.

However, in 1939, Tohata and Ohkawa identified problems with the original data (statistics produced by the Government-General of Korea) and recalculated the values, publishing them in a supplemental edition. Specifically, the figure for annual per capita rice consumption in 1930–33 was revised upward to 0.6203 *koku* and that in 1934–36 was calculated at 0.5839 *koku*. The authors thus concluded that, although it was still true that a reduction in rice consumption occurred, it was not as drastic as previously believed (Tohata and Ohkawa 1939, 428). This revised conclusion, however, went almost unnoticed.

The figures in the supplemental edition were problematic as well, because they underestimated the Korean population for the period 1915–19, which resulted in an inflated estimate of per capita rice consumption during that time. When this is taken into account, the rate of subsequent decline becomes even smaller. Recent research sets per capita rice consumption (*koku*) as follows: 1915–19, 0.589; 1930–33, 0.556; 1934–36, 0.511; and 1936–40, 0.555 (Kim Nak-nyeon 2006, 570). These figures indicate that there was only a slight decline in per capita rice consumption during the period in question. According to the same research, annual per capita consumption of all grains (rice, wheat, barley, other grains, and beans) declined slightly between 1910 and 1940, but when potatoes, vegetables, meat, fish, shellfish, and other foods are added, the per capita calories consumed declined very little (Kim Nak-nyeon 2006, 222).

The research did not cover trends from 1941 onward because of a lack of adequate data, but it is certain that per capita calorie intake declined substantially from 1941. I discuss this in more detail in chapter 4.

Per Capita Personal Consumption Expenditure

Food consumption is not the only element that determines a person's standard of living. Clothing and other manufactured consumption goods, housing, transportation, education, medical services, and other factors must also be considered. To discern changes in these many forms of consumption, we must evaluate their respective market values and sum up personal consumption expenditures.

Diverse consumer industries developed in Korea under Japanese rule. Modern manufactured products were introduced from Japan, and railways, roads, and communication networks were constructed. This resulted in an increase in the total amount of personal consumption. The question is whether or not this increase was greater than the growth rate of the population. Research up to now indicates that total personal consumption expenditure (in real terms) increased at a rate exceeding 3 percent per year from the 1910s through the 1930s. Because the population growth rate was lower than this, per capita consumption increased.

Looking in more detail, we see that per capita consumption expenditure increased at an average annual rate of 0.97 percent from 1912 to 1938 (Umemura and Mizoguchi 1988, 61). More recent research raises this figure to 1.94 percent (Kim Nak-nyeon 2006, 219). These two studies found minor differences in the growth rate of overall consumption expenditure, but the latter adopted a lower estimate of the population growth rate, which consequently resulted in a higher per capita consumption growth rate. The values in Japan (1.50%) and Taiwan (1.11%) were both lower during the same period.

Quality of Consumption, Government Services, and Distribution

Several points need to be considered for the estimates given above. First, a person's standard of living is determined not only by quantity but by quality. As we saw in the previous chapter, for example, the varieties of rice cultivated in Korea changed substantially under Japanese rule, resulting in a shift to varieties that people enjoyed more. Similarly, advances in husking and polishing techniques reduced the amount of impurities in rice. As a result, satisfaction (or what economists call "utility") increased for consumers even if they consumed the same quantity of rice as before. This factor improves the standard of living but is not reflected in the data shown above.

Second, there is the question of governmental services. The Government-General opened primary schools throughout Korea, and many Korean children (about 1 million at the end of the 1930s) began attending them. With the exception of tuition fees paid by parents or guardians, the expenses associated with primary education are not included in personal consumption expenditure. Educational content was focused primarily on practical courses that were beneficial for social life. Today, there are some in Japan who mistakenly believe that the use of the Korean language was prohibited in Korean schools under Japanese rule. But Hangul was a required course for many years, and it was not until 1938, after the start of the wartime period, that the Korean language became an elective. Many Korean children, especially girls who had almost no educational opportunities during the Korean dynasty period, learned Hangul in schools established by the Government-General. This practical education, including the learning of Hangul, must have served to enhance the satisfaction of the Korean people. However, the Government-General did make Japanese the national language of Korea and pushed assimilation as the basic educational policy, which was an affront to Korean ethnic dignity, so there is ample room for debate on just how much education under Japanese rule contributed to greater satisfaction among Koreans.

Government services designed to enhance public safety provide a similar example. These are also not included in calculations of personal consumption, but the protection of citizens through the application of laws and policing heightens public satisfaction. But what about the fact that these services were provided by people of a different ethnic group? Protection from robbery or corrupt public officials can undeniably be counted as a positive, but what about the banning of social unrest arising from anti-Japanese sentiments? The authorities no doubt viewed it as an appropriate measure, but those being restricted perceived it as unjust oppression. Evaluation of such policies differs depending on the position and values of each individual.

Some government services, however, such as those associated with hygiene and disinfection, are clearly factors that improve the general standard of living. Great strides were made in these fields under Japanese rule. For example, though it tends to be forgotten today, smallpox existed in both Japan and Korea from ancient times and occasionally a large outbreak would result in an epidemic. In 1895, near the end of the Korean dynasty period, the government began providing vaccinations as a national policy designed to prevent mass infection. Under Japanese rule, the Government-General further disseminated vaccines, making them mandatory in 1923. As a result, the number of Koreans who received vaccinations rose to several million per year in the 1920s and 1930s (each person received multiple vaccinations). The Government-General adopted policies to counteract not only such acute infectious diseases as smallpox, dysentery, typhoid, and cholera, but also chronic diseases such as paragonimiasis (caused by the parasitic lung fluke). Expenses for these health programs are again not included in calculations of personal consumption.

Third, there is the question of distribution. The figures for per capita consumption are only averages and do not directly indicate the consumption levels of the general population. If distribution becomes more unequal, the average values can rise but actual consumption levels for the majority of people could still decline. As I discussed in the Introduction, hardly any ordinary Koreans ate rice in the early period under consideration. This greatly reduces the significance of debating trends in per capita rice consumption amounts. It is difficult to verify patterns of distribution because data are limited. Therefore, I take a different approach to investigate changes in the general standard of living in the next section.

3. Changes in Body Height

Using Height Data to Illuminate the Standard of Living

Genetic makeup and habitat both have a strong influence on body height. Therefore, if we examine individuals or groups of people who have similar genetic makeups, we can surmise differences in habitat. Recently, economic historians in Europe and North America have increasingly experimented with using data on height to track historical changes in the standard of living. For example, researchers have long wrestled with the question of whether or not the Industrial Revolution led to a decline in the living standards of the British working class. Studies on height have cast new light on this topic.

It is widely recognized that, because of improvements in habitats for children that accompanied economic growth (particularly the rapid economic growth of the postwar period), the average height of the Japanese increased substantially. In postwar South Korea, as well, average height increased notably. In contrast, dwarfism among North Koreans is increasing, clearly indicating that the nutritional condition of the North Korean people has deteriorated (Kim Yeong-hui 2014). We have no systematic official statistics that indicate changes in the height of the Korean people under Japanese rule. For many years, the Government-General of Korea showed little interest in the health and physical strength of the Koreans under their charge. This changed, however, in the late 1930s, when Japan began mobilizing Koreans as human resources during the war, making it necessary to know their average physical strength.

Men
The Government-General conducted a survey in 1938, focusing on young workers (members of Seinen-dan, a youth group) and students. The results were noted by region. According to these statistics, the average height of 20-year-old Korean men was as shown in table 3-1. Students, especially in the central region of the country, were taller than workers of the same age. At the time, students were set apart from the general population and given elite treatment. One would expect their nutritional condition to be much better than average, and this is reflected in the height difference.

The tallest young workers were found in the north. The difference between them and young workers in the south is not great, but there is a noteworthy difference between young workers in the north and those in the central region. No great regional differences are discernable among students. Although there are many exceptions, there is a worldwide tendency for people (ethnic groups) in the north to be taller than those in the south. It is possible that Koreans had displayed this tendency before Japan assumed control.

In addition to the official survey noted above, several other surveys were conducted in the private sector. Most of these were not done on a large scale, but because the heights were measured by doctors, medical students, anthropologists, and others for scientific purposes, they are considered to be highly reliable and precise. Table 3-2 shows the results of surveys conducted at around the same time as that of the Government-General, dividing the subjects into age groups.

In 1940, Tanaka Masashi (and students in the medical department of Keijo Imperial University) measured heights of residents of slums in Seoul who were born in Gyeonggi-do and Chungcheong-do in the central region. The average height of men in their twenties was 161.22 centimeters, higher than that of young workers from the central region in the survey of the Government-General, but the difference was only about one centimeter. No notable difference is apparent in the respective heights of slum residents of different ages.

In 1937, Mikamo Masataka measured heights of long-term prison inmates. The location(s) of the prison(s) and the birthplaces of the subjects were not reported. Because Mikamo was affiliated with Keijo Imperial University, we can assume that Seoul was the surveyed area and that his incarcerated subjects were primarily from Gyeonggi-do and nearby provinces. The average height of subjects in their twenties surveyed by Mikamo is nearly the same as that of young workers from the central region in the survey of the Government-General. Virtually no difference was found in the respective heights of subjects of different ages in the Mikamo survey as well. With the exception of subjects in their thirties, the average height of each age group in the Mikamo survey

Table 3-1.

Average Height (cm) of 20-Year-Old Males, 1938

	South	Central	North
Working youth	162.3 (1,953)	160.2 (944)	163.4 (931)
Students	163.8 (684)	165.2 (347)	165.2 (440)

Note: Figures in parentheses indicate number of subjects surveyed.
Source: Kimura 1991, 209.

Table 3-2.

Average Height of Men by Age, 1937 and 1940

Researcher	Mikamo Masataka	Tanaka Masashi et al. (medical students at Keijo Imperial University)
Survey year	**1937**	**1940**
Subjects	Long-term prison inmates	Slum residents
Age	**Height (cm)**	**Height (cm)**
20–29	160.58 (230)	161.22* (89)
30–39	159.84 (347)	161.47 (70)
40–49	160.58 (263)	161.25 (67)
50–59	159.59 (115)	160.10 (55)
Overall	160.19 (955)	161.07 (281)

Note: Figures in parentheses indicate number of subjects surveyed. *Age 19-29
Source: Kimura 1991, 210.

nearly matches that in the Tanaka survey.

The Tanaka and Mikamo surveys have many points in common. They exhibit no evidence of changes in habitat that would significantly impact people's height between, for example, the period when the subjects in their twenties were born and raised (from the late 1910s till 1930s) and the period when the subjects in their forties were born and raised (prior to the late 1910s).

Table 3-3 shows the results of other surveys carried out in the 1930s. The survey conducted by Himeno Yukio and Yi In-gyu in 1930–31 and that by Yi Byeong-nam in 1938 targeted subjects who sought entry into technical schools in Seoul, so they probably can be considered to be part of the elite. Their average height of about 166 centimeters was exceptionally tall.

Table 3-3.

Average Height of Men in the 1930s

Researcher	Himeno Yukio and Yi In-gyu	Arase Susumu et al.	Arase Susumu et al.	Ueda Tsunekichi et al.	Yi Byeong-nam
Survey year	1930–31	1930	1930–31	1935–36	1938
No. of subjects	868	505	1,023	672	831
Average height (cm)	165.98	165.17	162.75	161.80	166.25
Age of subjects	18–23	20 and older (mostly 50 or younger)	Unknown (probably 20–50)	20 and older (mostly 60 or younger)	20–26
Birthplace	Unknown	Pyeongan-do, Hamgyeong-do	Provinces other than Pyeongan-do and Hamgyeong-do	Gyeonggi-do	Unknown
Occupation, etc.	Applicants seeking to enter technical schools in Seoul	About half were non-farmers, including students	Unknown	Unknown	Applicants seeking to enter technical schools in Seoul

Source: Kimura 1991, 211.

The other three surveys, which targeted subjects with wide-ranging ages, are flawed in that they made no attempt to distinguish between age groups. Even so, they relay some interesting facts. First, about half of the subjects surveyed by Arase Susumu et al. in 1930 were students and other non-farmers, setting them apart from the general population. Their average height exceeded 165 centimeters. Second, the survey conducted by Arase et al. in 1930–31 did not specify occupation, but it is probable that the subjects had a composition similar to that of the 1930 survey. The average height of subjects in the later survey was about 2.5 centimeters shorter. There was a difference in the geographical location of the subjects, with the 1930 survey focusing on the north and the 1930–31 survey focusing on the central and southern regions. This regional difference in average height is consistent with the difference found in the previously discussed Government-General survey. Third, the subjects of the survey by Ueda Tsunekichi et al. in 1935–1936 came from Gyeonggi-do. Although their occupations are not specified, their average height was extremely close to the overall average height of the slum residents noted in table 3-2.

Table 3-4.

Average Height of Men Prior to Annexation

Researcher	Migita Guntaro and Otsuka Rikutaro		Iijima Shigeru		Kubo Takeshi
Survey year	1895		1900-01		1909
No. of subjects	60	132	1,847	2,527	546
Average height (cm)	162.7	162.4	163.41	163.46	161.39
Age of subjects	19–30	19–55	21–30	21–60	20–35
Birthplace	Pyeongan-do, Hwanghae-do		Mostly north of Chungcheongbuk-do		Mostly Gyeonggi-do
Occupation, etc.	Unknown (probably soldiers and military support personnel)		Mostly low-ranking soldiers		low-ranking soldiers

Source: Kimura 1991, 211.

Three different surveys were conducted before annexation (1895, 1900–01, and 1909; table 3-4). The surveys by Iijima Shigeru and Kubo Takeshi both used low-ranking soldiers as subjects, who at that time were in low social classes. Most of the subjects in Iijima's survey came from the north, whereas most of those in Kubo's were from Gyeong-gi-do. The average height found in Iijima's survey was about 2 centimeters higher than that in Kubo's. This reflects the same regional differences cited in the previous surveys.

The subjects of the survey by Migita Guntaro and Otsuka Rikutaro were men from the north (Pyeongan-do and Hwanghae-do). Their occupations are unknown, but both Migita and Otsuka were military doctors working in the field, so it is likely that their subjects were soldiers and military support personnel. We can at least say that the subjects were not elite or people with high incomes. Their average height was close to that found in the Iijima survey.

Comparing these earlier surveys to the ones conducted in 1930–40, we find that the average height of subjects in the Iijima survey was about the same as that of northern young workers in the survey by the Government-General. In addition, there was no large difference between the average height reported in the Kubo Takeshi survey and the average heights of young workers from the central region (the Government-General, table 3-1), slum residents (Tanaka et al., table 3-2), and prison inmates (Mikamo, table 3-2).

In sum, average heights varied according to social class and geographic region, but not particularly by age or time period.

Women

Even though data are less available on the height of women, there are some surveys we can discuss. The first was produced in 1940 as part of the previously cited survey of slum residents, which categorized subjects according to age (table 3-5). The results show that subjects in their twenties were the tallest, with subjects in their thirties and forties successively shorter. However, subjects in their fifties were slightly taller than those in their forties, being about the same height as subjects in their thirties.

Four other data sets are shown in table 3-6. Of these, Go Nam-yeong and Shin Ung-ho report an extremely high average height of 151.6 centimeters. Their subjects were women who received outpatient care at Keijo Imperial University Hospital. Patients who could visit the university hospital at that time belonged to the middle class and higher. From the results in the other surveys already discussed, it is no surprise that this subset of subjects exhibited a relatively high average height.

Other surveys conducted in the 1930s focused on residents from the central region (Gyeonggi-do in particular). The subjects of Ueda Tsunekichi et al. were aged 35 and older. Their occupations and social class are unknown, but their average height (148.66 centimeters) is comparable to that of the slum residents in their thirties or older surveyed in 1940 (148.3 centimeters; table 3-5). The subjects of the survey by Gokita Jiro and Ikeda Katsuzo were prostitutes and female factory workers in their early twenties from Gyeonggi-do. They had about the same average height as the slum residents in their twenties previously referenced. These two surveys show consistent results. The Kubo survey is a valuable study of the early years. Although the sample does not include female factory workers, its subjects were prostitutes from Gyeonggi-do, so the sample overlaps somewhat with that used by Gokita and Ikeda. The average height reported by Kubo is lower than that in the Gokita

Table 3-5.

Average Height, According to Age, of Female Slum Residents, 1940

Age	Height (cm)
19–29	149.53 (138)
30–39	148.55 (131)
40–49	147.89 (82)
50–59	148.54 (45)
Average	148.75 (396)

Note: Figures in parentheses indicate number of subjects surveyed.
Source: Kimura 1991, 212.

and Ikeda survey.

Because the data sets are so small, it is difficult to draw clear conclusions about changes in average female height. One thing we can say, however, is that there is no evidence that it decreased with the passage of time.

The foregoing discussion is based on prewar data I collected in the early 1990s. Since then, Korean scholars have debated changes in the heights of Koreans under Japanese rule using newly found data sets. I will not go into detail, but recent research does not confirm the proposition that the average height of Koreans generally declined under Japanese rule (Ju 2005, 340). One of the studies found an even more positive result; that is, it found growth in the height of Korean males, which suggests an improving general standard of living (Kim and Park 2011).

Table 3-6.

Average Height of Women in 1909 and the 1930s

Researcher	Kubo Takeshi	Gokita Jiro and Ikeda Katsuzo	Ueda Tsunekichi et al.	Go Nam-yeong and Shin Ung-ho
Survey year	1909	1934	1935-36	Around 1937
No. of subjects	169	370	342	500
Average height (cm)	147.31	148.70	148.66	151.62
Age of subjects	18–32	18–23	35 and older (mostly 60 or younger)	20–40
Birthplace	Mostly Gyeonggi-do	Mostly Gyeonggi-do	Gyeonggi-do	Unknown
Occupation, etc.	Prostitute	Prostitute, textile factory worker	Unknown	Women who received outpatient care at the hospital at Keijo Imperial University

Source: Kimura 1991, 212.

Column 2.

How Korean History Textbooks Characterize Rice Consumption

History textbooks used in South Korea continue to highlight the "drastic decline" of per capita rice consumption as a symbol of Japan's misrule of Korea. The high school history textbook (*guksa*) issued by the South Korean government in 2006 includes a table showing amounts of production, exports, and per capita consumption of rice in Korea for every two years from 1912 to 1930. According to that data, average per capita rice consumption stood at 0.772 *koku* in 1912 and fell to 0.451 *koku* by 1930. The system of government-issued textbooks was subsequently abolished in favor of a system where the books were approved by the government, which led to the publication of different Korean history textbooks (*hanguksa*) by several private companies. All of the latest textbooks published by these companies base their information on the statistics of the Government-General of Korea. They state that per capita rice consumption dropped precipitously from 0.63 *koku* in 1920 to 0.45 *koku* in 1930.

As I have discussed here, the statistics of the Government-General were flawed and later corrected by Tohata and Ohkawa. Despite the fact that those corrections were made as early as 1939, and that additional research has been done on this issue both in Japan and South Korea after the war, no revision has been made to the original data in South Korea's history textbooks. Therefore, the spurious argument concerning rice consumption under Japanese rule has continued to be propagated in Korean society.

Textbooks referred:
Mitsuhashi Hiroo, trans., *Kankoku no koko rekishi kyokasho: Koto gakko kokutei kokushi* (South Korea's High School History Textbook: The National History of Korea in High Schools) (Akashi Shoten, 2006); and

textbooks published by five different publishers with the title *Godeung hakgyo hanguksa* (High School Korean History), which were certified by the Korean Ministry of Education in 2013 (publisher, year of publication): Donga Chulpansa, 2016; Bisang Gyoyuk, 2016; Geumseong Chulpansa, 2016; Mirae, 2016; and Jihaksa, 2017.

CHAPTER
4

Rapid Transition to the Wartime Economy
From the Sino-Japanese War until the Fall of the Empire

After the Sino-Japanese War (*Nicchu-senso*) (called by the Japanese at the time the "North China Incident" [*Hokushi-jihen*] and later the "China Incident" [*Shina-jihen*]) erupted in 1937, the Japanese Empire adopted a war system (*senji-taisei*), followed by a total war system (*soryoku-sen-taisei*). In the total war system, the government gave top priority to expanding production in all sectors and took all necessary measures to achieve it, especially in military-related industries. The main focus was strengthening state control over the economy both within Japan itself and in Korea. The administration of the Government-General of Korea accordingly shifted from a peace-time footing to a wartime one. That transition was so massive that it can be called all-encompassing. This being so, it is inappropriate to define Japanese rule in Korea in general terms without considering the differences in time periods. We cannot discuss wartime (indeed, a time of total war) and peace time as if they were equivalent.

This chapter discusses state control of agriculture and industry in Korea, and traces how industry was militarized. To begin, I summarize changes in the administrative structure and public finances of the Government-General of Korea in the late 1930s.

1. The Expansion of the Government-General

Rapid Increase in the Number of Korean Bureaucrats

The Government-General grew even larger after 1935. In the central government, the Home Affairs Bureau was divided into the General Affairs Bureau and the General Administration Bureau, an arrangement that lasted until September 1943 and brought the total number of bureaus to eight. The greatest increase was seen in the number of affiliated government offices, which rose to 41 by 1943. Many of the newly established offices were related to public safety and the military (including the Public Prosecutors' Office, Probation Office, Preventive Detention Center, Prison Officer Training Center, Military Volunteers Training Center, and Disabled Veteran Care Center).

In December 1943, entering the period of *kessen-taisei* (preparedness for the decisive battle), the Government-General was streamlined and centralized with the aim of increasing food production and thoroughly utilizing both material and human resources. The General Affairs, Judicial Administration, Industrial, and Agriculture and Forestry Bureaus were eliminated, and their main duties were taken over by the Agricultural Commerce Bureau and the Mining and Industrial Bureau. Among affiliated offices, the Railway Bureau was reorganized as the Transportation Bureau and given overall jurisdiction not only over land transport but also sea and air transport (formerly administered by the Communications Bureau), harbors (Judicial Administration Bureau), and customs (Financial Bureau).

The number of government employees exploded, exceeding 100,000 by 1942, an increase of 50 percent compared with 1937. The rate of increase was much higher than the increase of 27 percent in the five years before 1937. In 1942, the Government-General employed 57,000 Japanese nationals (an increase of 40 percent compared with 1937) and 46,000 Koreans (an increase of 90 percent). From this, we can see that many more Koreans joined the administrative structure during the war than had previously been the norm.

Budgetary Expansion

From 1937, the Government-General quickly swelled its tax revenue by introducing the North China Incident special tax and a provisional income tax, and by increasing the income tax and various indirect taxes (table 4-1). At the same time, its revenue from public bonds greatly increased. In 1937, the debt ceiling was raised substantially, and bond issues exceeded 100 million yen by 1939. From 1941, the Japanese government was issuing bonds to the Government-General of Korea to finance not only railway construction and infrastructure improvement but also anti-aircraft installations, the Food Corporation, and other entities with the aim of increasing production of rice and other goods.

On the spending side, drastic increases occurred in general expenditures, costs associated with government-run enterprises, and debt servicing (table 4-2). Increases in general expenditures were particularly notable near the end of the war, mainly because of large budgetary increases needed for the prosecution of the war, including increased food and mining production. Another reason for the increased budget was the increase in government employees and payments equivalent to "overseas allowances" to Korean bureaucrats. Originally, these allowances were special compensation paid to Japanese bureaucrats who had to leave Japan to serve. This resulted in Japanese employees earning more than their Korean counterparts for comparable work. The system came under criticism for being discriminatory against Koreans. With the idea of achieving "Japan and Korea as one" (*naisen-ittai*), the

Table 4-1.

**Annual Revenue of the Government-General:
Taxes, Subsidies, and Bonds, 1937–43**

(1,000 yen)

	Taxes						Subsidies	Bonds
	Total	Land taxes	Tariffs	Liquor taxes	Income taxes	Provisional Income taxes		
1937	86,413	13,827	12,801	24,067	16,590	2,840	12,914	51,004
1938	114,491	13,892	16,761	26,492	23,776	7,902	12,909	86,320
1939	150,230	9,950	17,231	28,059	35,599	21,589	12,904	134,018
1940	205,004	13,943	14,903	24,598	50,358	36,702	14,678	156,866
1941	242,386	14,105	7,765	31,344	65,147	47,370	12,944	149,109
1942	338,331	13,086	2,436	28,254	82,327	67,164	12,967	166,673
1943	368,709	21,594	2,333	47,616	78,763	58,713	12,957	379,195

Note: The figures are settled amounts for all fiscal years except 1943; figures for 1943 are budget amounts. The total exceeds the sum of the listed taxes because not all tax categories are shown.
Sources: The Government-General of Korea, *Chosen Sotokufu tokei nempo* (each relevant year) and Chosen Ginko Chosabu 1948, III, 113.

Government-General raised the compensation to Korean employees to match that of the Japanese employees in 1944–45.

Expenditures for maintaining public order also increased as police duties multiplied to include counterintelligence, air defense, firefighting, flood prevention, and administrative duties related to military volunteers. In addition, state control of the economy engendered a thriving black market, the crackdown of which required further resources (an Economic Police Section was established within the Police Bureau in 1940). Compared with the rate of increased expenditures in these areas, however, the increase in other general expenditures was far larger, so that costs associated with public order and safety actually declined as a percentage of total general expenditures.

As the Sino-Japanese War expanded, the Japanese government established the Special Account for Extraordinary Military Spending in

Table 4-2.

Annual Expenditures of the Government-General, 1937–45

(1,000 yen)

	General expenditures		Government-run enterprises	Servicing debt	Extraordinary military spending	Total
	Total	Maintaining public order				
1937	144,995	36,150	239,330	29,764	11,034	425,123
1938	162,518	37,637	307,040	31,709	26,978	528,245
1939	216,189	40,759	414,285	35,219	42,291	707,984
1940	296,749	41,833	477,727	41,683	50,482	866,641
1941	362,063	50,843	555,661	48,409	94,568	1,060,701
1942	393,950	55,477	513,013	54,542	163,212	1,124,717
1943	721,121	55,716	684,559	63,227	203,058	1,671,965
1944	1,018,109	69,230	927,344	82,178	414,075	2,441,706
1945	1,431,119	101,992	970,608	109,167	606,213	3,117,107

Note: The figures are budget amounts for each fiscal year.
Sources: The Government-General of Korea, *Chosen Sotokufu tokei nempo* (each relevant year); Chosen Ginko Chosabu 1948, III, 113; The Government-General of Korea 1999, 518–519; and Mizuta 1974a, 117, 121.

September 1937, to which the Government-General of Korea transferred funds from its account. After annexation, Korea was not called upon to pay for the imperial military until the start of the Sino-Japanese War. The transferred amount increased rapidly from 1937 to 1945.

Public finances also expanded on the local level, the largest of which were related to the provinces. Provincial expenditures increased rapidly from 70 million yen in 1935 to 170 million yen in 1940 and to 260 million yen in 1943. This increase was mainly attributable to increases in civil engineering expenses and subsidies earmarked for industry and education.

In the late 1930s, railway operations moved into the black because of a rapid increase in freight transport revenue due to the more active distribution of goods. Current revenue greatly outpaced interest payments (Hirai 1997, 149–176). In this respect, the Government-General gained from the development of the wartime economy.

2. The Food Production Increase Plan and State Control of Agriculture

Movement to Mobilize and Organize Agricultural Labor

As discussed in chapter 2, the Sanmai Zoshoku Keikaku (Rice Production Development Program), which was first introduced in Korea in 1920, had been discontinued in all but name by the early 1930s because of a slump in the agricultural economy. By 1939, however, such plans were resuscitated in Korea to take their place alongside similar campaigns implemented in Japan and Taiwan.

A more concrete, long-term plan was developed in 1940 with the aim of increasing, over the course of six years until 1945, rice production by 4.63 million *koku* through improvements in cultivation techniques (primarily through the increased use of fertilizer and seed renewal) and by 1.2 million *koku* through land improvements (primarily the development of new fields through the installation of irrigation systems, the adjustment of existing cultivated fields, etc.). In 1942, the Government-General expanded these programs and greatly raised the targeted production increase to 12 million *koku* over 12 years. Emphasizing land improvement in the new plan, the Government-General established the Chosen Nochi Kaihatsu Eidan (Korea Farmland Development Corporation) in August 1943 as the implementing agency. The corporation was charged with improving a total of about 577,000 *chobu* (1 *chobu* = 0.992 hectares) of farmland, far more than the 244,300 *chobu* designated for improvement under the Sanmai Zoshoku Keikaku in the 1920s. Programs to increase the production of barley and other crops were also formulated during this time.

To realize increased production, the Government-General encouraged the organization and mobilization of farmers. In October 1940, it established the Kokumin Soryoku Chosen Renmei (Korean Federation for National Total Mobilization), which worked in conjunction with the Taisei Yokusan-kai (Imperial Rule Assistance Association). This Federation was a reorganization of the Kokumin Seishin Sodoin Chosen Renmei (Korean Federation of National Spiritual Mobilization, founded in 1938), and it worked to transform the Rural Revitalization Campaign (Noson Shinko Undo), which started in the early 1930s, into the Rural and Mountain Village Production and Patriotism Campaign (Nosanson Seisan Hokoku Undo). The Federation also supervised village federations organized in more than 70,000 villages (all farmers were required to be members). The village federations were based on traditional mutual financing organizations for individual farmers (*shokusankei*, equivalent to *tanomoshiko* in Japan), which were reorganized as corporations in 1930. They became front-line agents for implementing plans to increase production.

For a three-year period starting in 1941, Village Production Expansion Projects were planned that assigned production targets for various crops to each farmer. In April 1942, Regulations on the Planting of Farmland in Korea were enacted, which prohibited the planting of non-food crops in cultivated fields for food crops. In 1944, the Government-General, prior to the central government in Japan, formulated Guidelines for Implementing a System of Responsibility for Agricultural Production to push policies for increased production. Crops targeted by these regulations included not just food grains but also crops like cotton and hemp for industrial use, livestock, and straw products such as woven mats and bags.

Spiritual mobilization programs for increased production were propelled through such movements as the Youth Production and Patriotism Campaign, with the interspersion of military terms such as "farmer-warrior," "full march ahead," and "full charge movement" that encouraged more aggressive development.

Efforts were made to increase fertilizer production as well. Because there were limits to increases in chemical fertilizer production, emphasis was placed on self-supplied fertilizer (compost, green manure, and liquid fertilizer), with promotional programs put in place in all villages.

Because the realization of increased farm products required large inputs of labor, and Korean youth had already been mobilized for working in mines and factories, the Government-General began to recognize the lack of agricultural labor. As a countermeasure, it issued Guidelines for Agricultural Labor Adjustment to all provinces in 1941. The intention was to break through workforce restrictions by elevating the working spirit of the people, organizing and communalizing agricultural labor, establishing and expanding common farming facilities, redistributing cultivated land among farming households, and mobilizing female workers.

In response, villages formed cooperative groups keyed to different kinds of cultivation activity (such as plowing with oxen) so that such tasks as plowing, planting, irrigating, weeding, harvesting, and produce preparation were carried out not by single households but jointly among several households. In the final stage of the war, a policy was formulated to create "military-style organized production-increase corps" with the goal of organizing each village or neighborhood association as a unit.

In addition, people of all classes belonging to all groups were mobilized to participate in communal agricultural work for the sake of increased production.

Control of Distribution and Consumption

In 1939, the Government-General issued the Korean Rice Ration Adjustment Ordinance and Notification Concerning the Control of Rice Rations, which brought Korean rice under full-fledged state control by initiating the regulation of prices, distribution, and collection. From that point on, rice began to be delivered forcibly to the government for the purpose of supply-demand adjustment within Korea, on the basis of official, maximum pricing.

A large number of entities were established to implement the regulations, including Chosen Beikoku Shijo Kabushiki Kaisha, Chosen Ryokoku Kabushiki Kaisha, Do Ryokoku Kabushiki Kaisha, Do Ryokoku Haikyu Kumiai, and Chosen Ryokoku Chuo Haikyu Kumiai. In 1943, with the aim of strengthening state control of cereal grain production and distribution, the Korean Foodstuffs Control Special Account Act and Korean Foodstuffs Management Ordinance were issued. At the same time, Chosen Beikoku Shijo Kabushiki Kaisha and Do Ryokoku Kabushiki Kaisha merged to form Chosen Shokuryo Eidan (Korea Foodstuffs Corporation).

Regulation was relatively lax at first but became increasingly strict, to the point that farmers were required to store and deliver rice on demand. With the promulgation of the Foodstuff Measure for Rice-year 1941, the Government-General prohibited any sales of rice before mandated delivery was complete. The basic steps in this policy were as follows: 1) at the beginning of the year, the Government-General set the annual per capita amount of rice to be consumed throughout Korea and provided each province with its quota by multiplying that amount by the number of residents in each province; 2) these amounts were compared with the amounts of rice produced, and provinces with an excess or a shortfall were identified; and 3) excess rice was placed under the control of the Government-General and supplied to provinces with shortfalls, exported to Japan, and delivered to meet the demand from non-farming households in Korea.

The amount earmarked for mandated delivery increased year by year. By 1943, virtually all of the rice under state control was procured through mandated delivery. The free sale of rice was prohibited to all but specially designated buyers. Minor grains and other farm products were also subjected to mandated delivery. Delivery was implemented by agricultural associations and other organizations (including municipal cereal grain delivery committees and village delivery implementation groups). Ultimately, responsibility for final delivery rested with the village federations.

The regulation of consumption also grew stricter over time. Plans were formulated by each administrative unit with the aim of reducing rice consumption and promoting the substitution of other foods. All grains over the amount deemed necessary for farmers (i.e., the self-stored amount) became subject to mandated delivery. In 1942, in the plains of Hwanghae-do in the western part of northern Korea, farmers were allowed to keep one *koku* of unhusked rice per person and were required to deliver the rest of their crop to the government. The plan for rice year 1944 allocated a per capita stored amount of 0.607 *koku* for farmers throughout Korea. However, the actual amount of rice consumed per farmer in that year fell below 0.4 *koku*. This was because the actual yield fell far below the planned yield in that year, but the decline was not fully reflected in a comparable reduction in mandated delivery.

To strengthen state control, it was necessary to obtain more accurate statistics on production and consumption. The Government-General therefore implemented detailed surveys to ascertain the labor force, agricultural implements, planting area for each crop, fertilizer production and consumption, and other factors of production for each household. To get accurate data of harvested yield, it also introduced *tsubogari-ho*, a method of on-site measuring of the yield per *tsubo* (about 3.3 m^2) of land, for rice in 1936 and for barley and wheat in 1942.

Changes in Landownership:
The Dismantling of Private Ownership and
Rise of Collective Ownership

In prewar years, the Government-General assured the privileges of landowners (both Japanese and Korean) and used their influence to rule over rural Korea. During the wartime period, however, landowners were not spared the same strict controls that applied to others.

In 1939, the Government-General promulgated the Ordinance for Controlling Tenancy Rent, which prohibited landowners from freely changing the rent they charged tenant farmers. In 1941, an upper limit was placed on the selling price of agricultural land on the basis of the Temporary Control on Price of Agricultural Land Ordinance. Landowners were also ordered to deliver the rice they took from tenant farmers as rent. Like the order applying to farmers, this order grew more stringent over time. In May 1945, landowners were required to surrender to the government all of the rice they received from tenants except for three *go* (about 0.54 liter) per person per day for personal consumption. Under this system, the tenant farmers delivered the rice directly to the government, and the landowners merely received payment for it. Although the landowners nominally retained their dominant power over the tenant farmers, in practical terms, the Government-General largely usurped their right to freely use and dispose of the assets and profits that accrued from their ownership rights.

At the same time, the Government-General made landowners officially responsible for agricultural production, in contrast to the system practiced in Japan, which placed responsibility on the farmers who actually worked the land. The commonly held view is that this measure strengthened the landlord system in Korea, but in fact it represented a hollowing out of landownership rights. The aim of the Government-General was to force many absentee landlords and, more generally, landowners who had no interest in the farming business, to become positively engaged in production increases. Specifically, it was an attempt to convert landowners into production managers, effectively transforming them into a kind of working class with reduced ownership rights so that they would be mobilized for agricultural production.

As expansion of the war necessitated increased agricultural production and delivery at an ever-faster pace, landowners who did not contribute to production and merely skimmed off rent (intermediary exploitation of produce) did more harm than good. The Government-General thus hardened its position against all such landowners by defining them as absentee. Not only that, but it actually developed a policy to strip managerial rights from landowners who lacked managerial ability. This policy was first embodied in a system introduced in 1944 (earlier in certain regions) that took absentee landowners' managerial and operational rights and entrusted them to irrigation associations. To realize the radical policy of increasing annual food production by 850,000 *koku*, the Government-General pushed the introduction of this system throughout Korea. One of the first irrigation associations to implement this policy was located in Bupyeong, Gyeonggi-do, which took responsibility for managing fields belonging to 29 landowners, each owning over five *chobu* (for a total area of about 200 *chobu* cultivated by 370 tenant farmers) and succeeded in increasing both production and profits.

Labor Outflow and Decline in Production

The target of policies for agricultural land management also included so-called "underperforming farmers" (either tenant or owner), who were not very productive. In March 1944, the Government-General established Guidelines for Measures Concerning Agricultural Land Management and Underperforming Farmers, which stipulated that the lands of any farmer who was designated as underperforming should be either rented or transferred to appropriate farmers, village federations, or youth associations. Thus, the removal of underperforming owners and cultivators and the creation of a more efficient production and delivery system became an important national goal near the end of the war. The movement in that direction represented increased governmental intrusion in agricultural management and the creation of large-scale farms led by the state. The head of the Agricultural and Commerce Bureau of the Government-General had the following to say in February 1944: "Integrated management is ideal for increased production, and it is desirable for management associations to run the operation of a large-scale farmland system." This clearly indicates the policy adopted by the Government-General at the time. Experiments in this farmland management system soon ended with the defeat of the Japanese Empire, but in practical terms, they represented the first step toward land reform to overturn the existing system of landownership.

Meanwhile, the outflow of young and middle-aged workers from the agricultural to the mining and manufacturing sectors in Japan and Korea far exceeded the amount of agricultural labor that could be bolstered through systemic reorganization, collectivization, and female mobilization. Despite the utmost efforts made by the government, shortages of fertilizers and raw materials continued to intensify. Furthermore, excessive demands of the government for mandated delivery depressed farmers' incentive to work. As a result, agricultural production steeply declined in the 1940s. From 1940 through 1944, total annual foodstuff production (grains and potatoes) declined from 7.26 million to 6.80 million tons, or from 0.306 to 0.263 ton per capita (table 4-3).

Table 4-3.

Foodstuff Production, 1940–44

	1940	1941	1942	1943	1944
Total (1,000 tons)	7,261	7,536	5,276	6,225	6,802
Per capita (tons)	0.306	0.305	0.209	0.233	0.263
Amount of rice produced (1,000 tons)	3,229	3,733	2,353	2,808	2,451
Per capita (tons)	0.136	0.151	0.093	0.105	0.095

Note: The total amount includes rice, wheat and barley varieties, minor grains, legumes, and potatoes.
Source: Kimura 2016, 43.

3. Control of Industry and the "Peninsular Ministry of Munitions"

Control of Business Enterprises and the Move toward Nationalization

Six years after it was implemented in Japan, the Act Concerning the Control of Important Industries was promulgated in Korea in 1937, bringing into full force state control of all commercial and industrial activity. More control laws followed that affected transactions, prices, financing, wages, and other areas as a transition was made from a market economy to a controlled economy. In May 1942, the Re-Establishing Business Enterprises Ordinance came into force in Japan and was applied to Korea at almost the same time. Intended to boost the production capacity of strategic industries, this ordinance gave the government a legal foundation for directly intervening in company management, including such actions as banning the relocation and transfer of equipment and facilities, and ordering companies to commission work and carry out mergers.

Government-run enterprises such as the Chosen Jutaku Eidan (Korea Housing Corporation) (1941) and the Chosen Juyo Busshi Eidan (Korea Key Commodities Corporation) (1943) were established in key fields. The main activity of the Chosen Juyo Busshi Eidan was to buy, sell, and hold industrial facilities that were incomplete or idle. This included the purchase of assets of "currently non-essential small and medium companies" that had been ordered by the Government-General to convert or discontinue operations.

Similarly, as part of food control, the Chosen Shokuryo Eidan (mentioned earlier) bought the equipment and facilities of rice-polishing companies and put them under direct management. Specifically, it bought 500 rice-polishing plants in April 1944, integrated them, and began operating them directly. Thus, one of the mainstay industries in Korea was nationalized. The nationalization of private companies extended to the railways, as well. In 1943–44, the Government-General took over about 400 kilometers of private railway lines with the aim of strengthening the transport capacity for strategic commodities. This resulted in the transference of the main lines (in two cases, all the lines) operated by five private companies (including Chosen Tetsudo Kabushiki Kaisha) to government management.

In 1943, the Imperial Diet promulgated the Munitions Companies Act, which emphasized that companies should contribute not to the profits of shareholders but rather to the benefit of society. It also stipulated that the government had a strong right to lead and direct important private companies. Through this law, designated munitions companies became subject to production orders, with individuals designated as responsible parties for production and government monitors (munitions comptrollers) dispatched. The law also recognized the right of the government to prioritize the distribution of raw materials and financial resources to munitions companies, exempt munitions companies from the application of certain control ordinances, and grant subsidies and provide compensation for losses without Diet approval. In 1944, there were 149 designated munitions companies in Japan; by 1945, that number had increased to 688.

In April 1943, a system of responsibility for munitions production based on "moral responsibility" was implemented in Korea. In 1944, a year later than in Japan, the Munitions Companies Act was applied there. In December 1944, there were 31 designated munitions companies that had either head offices or branch offices located in Korea. These included Chosen Onoda Cement, Nippon Magnesium Kinzoku, Mitsui Yushi Kagaku, Mitsubishi Magnesium Kogyo, Chosen Chisso Kayaku, Chosen Kikai Seisakusho, Ryuzan Kosaku, and Chosen Seitetsu. In January 1945, Chosen Oryokuko Suiryoku Hatsuden (discussed below) was designated as a munitions company. Although designated munitions companies were formally defined as private companies pursuing profit, they were in fact very similar to government-run enterprises and subject to extremely strict government supervision and command. If production quotas were not met, the government could dismiss the designated person in charge (usually the CEO of the munitions company in question). This was not merely a regulatory provision. In Korea, the person responsible for production at one munitions company was actually discharged.

Control and Mobilization of Labor

In October 1943, the Government-General announced Guidelines on Measures for Increasing Production and Strengthening the Workforce. Designed to reinforce the National Requisition Ordinance that had already come into force, the guidelines focused on mobilizing idle and non-essential workers and included various measures, such as the following: expanding requisitions; strengthening the Labor Service Corps and organizing it according to occupation; mobilizing female workers; strengthening control over hiring, transferring, and firing workers; giving priority to supplying necessary materials to workers in key industries (special rations); procuring housing for workers; improving welfare facilities (healthcare, hygiene, procurement cooperatives, etc.); and increasing piece wages. In short, the Government-General implemented thorough measures to mobilize all workers (including women, who had previously not been under government control), heighten willingness to work, and improve efficiency.

At each factory and mine, "service corps" were formed. They were organized in a military fashion based on Workplace Associations and Local Patriotism Groups. The factory service corps comprised teams, sections, and squads, in descending order, and under this structure, workers were forced to obey all regulations and improve operating efficiency. Near the end of the war, two other kinds of organizations were formed at key mines and factories for the purpose of achieving emergency production increases: the Special Fighting Spirit Corps and the Commando Corps. Thus, every production site had some kind of military-style "corps" that mobilized workers at various levels to increase production.

"Peninsular Ministry of Munitions":
The Mining and Industries Bureau

As state control over industry tightened, economic planning was introduced into the imperial economy. The Cabinet Planning Board, which was established in Japan in 1937, became the driving force behind the Materials Mobilization Plan (a plan for allotting key resources). In 1943, the Cabinet Planning Board was absorbed by the Ministry of Munitions. In Korea, the Mining and Industries Bureau of the Government-General was created at the end of 1943 and given jurisdiction over the production and distribution of iron and steel, light metals, chemical products, and other key resources. In that capacity, it imposed quarterly and monthly production targets on major mines and factories. The Mining and Industries Bureau was nicknamed the "Peninsular Ministry of Munitions."

As production quotas were developed, resource shortages grew more severe and the term *airo* (bottleneck) came into use in both Japan and Korea to signify shortage. The setting of quantitative targets also led to a decline in product quality. Meanwhile, imbalances between different industrial sectors intensified, so that certain sectors experienced surpluses and waste even in the midst of overall shortages. These problems resulted from the loss of the resource allocation function of the market, because of the strict production and consumption quota system practiced in the imperial economy.

4. Military Industrialization:
Development into an Essential Region for Total War

Hydraulic Power: Supung Dam

In 1937, Noguch Shitagau founded Oryokuko Suiryoku Hatsuden Kabushiki Kaisha (Yalu River Hydroelectric Power Company) and began developing power generation on the main course of the Yalu River. Unlike the watershed modification project Noguchi undertook on the Bujeon River, this project entailed the construction of a giant dam in Supung (located on the lower reaches of the Yalu River), which could generate electricity by controlling water levels and releasing stored water. Engineers employed by Hazama Gumi and Nishimatsu Gumi, the two companies in charge of construction, went to inspect Hoover Dam and Grand Coulee Dam in the United States and introduced the construction techniques and equipment they encountered there. The project mobilized a total of 25 million workers, many of whom were recruited from rural areas in southern Korea.

The completed dam was 106 meters high and 900 meters long, making it one of the largest in the world at the time. The reservoir was about half as large as Lake Biwa (the largest lake in Japan) and supplied seven power plants. Assembly of the first generator (built by Tokyo Shibaura Denki), with a generating capacity of 100,000 kilowatts, was completed in 1941.

More hydroelectric plants were built on the Yalu and Tumen rivers after the Supung Dam was completed. Four power plants on the Jangjin River in Ganggye were built in mountain bedrock so that they could withstand air raids (the main contractors for these projects were Shimizu Gumi and Tobishima Gumi). However, the war ended just before these projects were completed, and all of the installed equipment was left onsite.

Development of the Mining Industry:
Basic Minerals, Rare Metals, and Uranium Ore

After 1930, the Government-General actively searched for minerals, either directly or by encouraging mining companies and Keijo Imperial University to do so. After war broke out between Japan and the United States, the scope of the search for new resources widened to meet the increased demand for munitions. In 1943, the Government-General created the Survey Group for the Emergency Development of Important Minerals in Korea, which comprised 35 teams that conducted surveys of mineral deposits. As a result, deposits of many rare minerals were discovered, particularly in northern Korea. These included cobalt, zircon, and other minerals that were difficult to find elsewhere in the Greater East Asia Co-Prosperity Sphere. Table 4-4 provides an outline of the rare minerals excavated or discovered in Korea.

Near the end of the war, the following minerals were mined in Korea on either an "extremely urgent" or "special emergency" basis: lead, molybdenum, fluorite, graphite, potassium feldspar, kotoite, tourmaline, lithium, columbite, and monazite. The production and development of these and other minerals are described below.

Anthracite

The yearly output of the Mining Division of the Naval Fuel Arsenal in Pyongyang increased to 180,000 tons by 1938. In 1941, the division was reorganized to become the Fifth Naval Fuel Arsenal. Its anti-aircraft and anti-fire facilities were expanded, with increased production of coal and briquettes. Near the end of the war, it excavated about 250,000 tons of coal per year, with four briquette factories that had an annual output of 250,000 tons.

During the 1940s, Chosen Muentan Kabushiki Kaisha continued to expand its facilities and increase production. In particular, it greatly increased supply to industries located in Korea. Its annual output of coal stood at 1.3 million tons in 1940 and 1.6 million tons in 1941. The output in 1945 is unknown, but the plan was to increase it to 3.1 million tons.

In 1938, a prominent industrialist in Korea named Arai Hatsutaro (born in Toyama Prefecture in 1868) and some others founded Choyo Kogyo. The company was capitalized at 5 million yen, (half of which was invested by Nihon Koshuha Jukogyo) and was dedicated to developing anthracite mines in the western part of northern Korea. The coal mined in these areas had low sulfur and ash content and was considered some of the best anthracite in Korea. It was prized in the steel and chemical sectors.

The Bongcheon coal mine in Gaecheon-gun, Pyeongannam-do (the

Table 4-4.

Uses and Distributions of Rare Minerals

Mineral or chemical substance	Ore in which it is found	Primary use	Main final products/ applications	Reserves (production locations)
Graphite	Vein graphite, earthy graphite	Electrodes, crucibles	Electric furnaces	One of the largest deposits in the world found in northern Korea (Pyeonganbuk-do)
Phosphorus	Apatite	Chemical materials	Phosphorus fertilizer, explosives	Mined in the eastern part of northern Korea. Large deposit discovered near the end of the war.
Silica	Silica sand	Chemical materials	Fireproof bricks, abrasives, glass	Plentiful throughout Korea
Silicon	Silica sand	Metal alloys, special steel	Transformers, power lines	
Boron (borax)	Kotoite, tourmaline	Chemical materials	Optical equipment, gunpowder, enameled ironware, welding	Kotoite deposit discovered in northern Korea (Hwanghae-do) near the end of the war
Magnesium	Magnesite, bittern	Metal alloys, chemical materials	Aircraft fuselages, fireproof bricks, flares, incendiary bombs	Large magnesite deposit in northern Korea (Hamgyeongnam-do)
Aluminum	Alunite, alumina shale, kaolin, nepheline	Metal alloys, chemical materials	Aircraft fuselages, instrument components, incendiary bombs	Large alunite deposit in southern Korea
Thorium, cerium, lanthanum, uranium	Monazite (heavy sand), allanite, columbite	Metal alloys, chemical materials, electrodes	Aircraft fuselages, paint, searchlights (carbon rods used for light sources), nuclear fuel	Plentiful in northern Korea
Molybdenum	Wulfenite	Special steel, chemical materials	High-grade tools, explosives, fuel	Productive mines in southern Korea (Jeollabuk-do)
Manganese	Manganese ore	Special steel, chemical materials	High-grade tools, gauges, pharmaceuticals	Mined in various areas but not plentiful

Mineral or chemical substance	Ore in which it is found	Primary use	Main final products/ applications	Reserves (production locations)
Barium	Barite	Metal alloys, chemical materials	Explosives, dyes, paper-making, photography, inks, glass, pharmaceuticals	Productive mines in northern Korea (the northern part of Gangwon-do)
Strontium	Barite	Chemical materials	Luminous paint, pyrotechnics, signal flares	
Nickel	Nickel ore	Special steel, metal alloys	Gun barrels, bullet jackets	Mined in northern Korea (Hamgyeongnam-do and the northern part of Gangwon-do)
Cobalt	Cobalt ore	Special steel, chemical materials	Aircraft fuselages, high-grade tools	Mined in northern Korea (Hamgyeongnam-do)
Tungsten	Tungsten ore	Special steel	High-grade tools, light machine guns, rifles, helmets, shields	Large deposits throughout Korea
Cadmium	Zinc ore	Metal alloys, chemical materials	Bearings, plating, pigments	Plentiful in northern Korea
Halogen	Fluorite, cryolite	Chemical materials	Ironmaking, aluminum smelting	Plentiful in northern Korea
Beryllium	Beryl	Special steel, chemical materials	High-grade tools, metallic reflectors, explosives, fuel	Mined throughout Korea
Zircon	Hyacinth, heavy sand	Special steel, chemical materials	High-grade tools, armor for tanks and naval vessels, aircraft fuselages, instrument components, explosives, fuel, refractories	Large deposit discovered in northern Korea (Hamgyeongbuk-do) during the war

Mineral or chemical substance	Ore in which it is found	Primary use	Main final products/ applications	Reserves (production locations)
Niobium, tantalum	Columbite, tantalite	Special steel, electrodes, chemical materials	Telecommunications equipment (vacuum tube anodes for VHF use), aircraft fuselages, high-grade tools, electric furnaces, special chemical machinery	One of the largest deposits in the world found in northern Korea (Pyeonganbuk-do)
Titanium	Rutile, ilmenite, black sand	Special steel, chemical materials	High-grade tools, welding, smoke generators	Mined in northern Korea
Lithium	Lepidolite, pyroxene	Metal alloys, chemical materials	Aircraft fuselages, fluorescent agents, incendiary bombs for target marking	Plentiful in northern Korea
Mica	Mica ore	Heat and electrical insulators	Instrument components	Mined throughout northern Korea
Asbestos	Serpentine, amphibole	Reinforcement fibers	Protective clothing, insulators, board-filling materials	Mined throughout Korea

Note: Final products and applications focus on military uses near the end of the war. "Halogen" is a generic term that includes fluorine, chlorine, bromine, iodine, and astatine; "niobium" is also called columbium. Reserves were estimated on the basis of wartime documents. The term "plentiful" is neither absolute nor fixed; it is a relative and fluid concept that changes depending on the degree of demand, available technology, and governmental policy. References to "large deposit discovered" do not necessarily mean discovery through exploration in a strict sense; it is possible that they only refer to promising observations made at the time.
Source: This table was compiled using various documents (for details, see Kimura and Abe 2003, 99).

western part of northern Korea), was known as the premier source of high-quality anthracite in Korea. Beginning in 1941, it was developed by Hosen Muentanko Kabushiki Kaisha (founded in 1934). The company engaged in strip mining as well as underground mining. Near the end of the war, the extracted coal was used to make steel in small blast furnaces. The Samcheok coal mine in southern Korea also expanded its facilities and increased its labor force beginning in 1940, thereby drastically increasing its output. To improve the quality of the mined coal, it installed Korea's first flotation coal-sorting equipment in 1942.

Soft (Smoky) Coal

During the war, there were more than 300 million tons of known soft coal deposits in northern Korea. The Sariwon coal mine, which was operated by Meiji Kogyo, produced an average of about 300,000 tons of brown coal annually from 1937 through 1941. The Anju coal mine, also operated by Meiji Kogyo, planned to increase production to 250,000 tons in 1945, and to 500,000 tons in 1946.

Chosen Yuentan Kabushiki Kaisha acquired three productive coal mines located in the eastern part of northern Korea in 1941. Each of these mines produced several tens of thousands of tons annually, most of which was sold to the Railway Bureau of the Government-General. The amount of soft coal deposits at mines owned by Chosen Yuentan was estimated at tens of millions of tons. In 1943, Dai-Nippon Boseki purchased and began operating the Gungsim coal mine in Hoeryeong, Hamgyeongbuk-do, in the eastern part of northern Korea. This mine, which opened in 1936, was one of the most prominent soft coal mines in Korea, and it was part of a large coal vein that extended into the Soviet Union and Manchuria. The coal was of good quality with a high caloric value (about 6,600 calories per gram). The initial monthly output was 8,000 tons, but the development of the surrounding mining area and additional purchases boosted production to 40,000 tons per month by 1944–45. The mined coal was intended for consumption by the Cheongjin Chemical Plant also owned by Dai-Nippon Boseki (discussed below), but in accordance with an order issued by the Government-General, 60 percent was supplied to the Railway Bureau and the rest divided among various companies.

Iron

Around 1930, Mitsubishi Kogyo (now Mitsubishi Materials Corporation) began full-fledged operations in Korea. One of its main focuses was the development of the Musan iron mine, located in Hamgyeong-buk-do in the northeastern part of northern Korea. At that time, the mine belonged to Mitsubishi Seitetsu. In 1934, Mitsubishi Seitetsu consolidated with Nippon Seitetsu, at which time the mine was turned over to Mitsubishi Kogyo. In 1939, ownership of the mine was transferred to Mosan Tekko Kaihatsu Kabushiki Kaisha, a company established with a capitalization of 50 million yen by Mitsubishi Kogyo, Nippon Seitetsu, and Nittetsu Kogyo. The establishment of Mosan Tekko Kaihatsu was promoted by Nippon Seitetsu, which needed iron ore for Cheongjin Ironworks. Thus, the Musan iron mine was acquired by Nippon Seitetsu but actually operated by Mitsubishi Kogyo.

From 1938 to 1941, Mitsubishi Kogyo invested 35 million yen in the Musan mine to construct ore-sorting facilities with an annual processing capacity of 2 million tons with a quality grade of 60 percent. The mining method entailed open-pit strip mining up to a depth of 15 meters, which required the introduction of many pieces of the latest large equipment from the United States. First, to break the ground, a large, self-propelled boring machine was used in conjunction with dozens of tons of explosives that blasted anywhere from several tens of thousands of tons to as much as 300,000 tons of ore at once. The broken ore was then collected by bulldozers and electric mining shovels with a maximum capacity of five tons, and loaded onto more than 10 giant dump trucks that could carry as much as 35 tons each at a time. The ore was then transported to the sorting and crushing plant. Large machinery was installed at the sorting station as well. Power for operating the machines and for heating, which was needed to avoid freezing during the winter, was supplied in large quantities by the Jangjin River Hydroelectric Power Plant located more than 100 kilometers away. To accommodate this, large-scale power-receiving equipment was installed. In short, the Musan mine possessed American-style high-performance, large-scale mining technology and facilities that were rarely found anywhere in the world at that time and inspired admiration in anyone who saw it.

Although the mine had an annual output of only 230,000 tons in 1940, it increased to 1 million tons in 1942 and to 1.05 million tons in 1944. Along with the Kamaishi and Anshan mines, the Musan mine was one of the largest mines operating in Japan, Manchuria, and Korea. The next largest mines in Korea were the Yiwon, Gaecheon, Yangyang, and Haseong iron mines, which had outputs ranging from 300,000 to 600,000 tons per year. These numbers highlight the massive scale of the Musan mine. However, annual production there never approached the 5 million tons initially anticipated. Most of the iron ore obtained at the Musan mine was sent to Nippon Seitetsu Cheongjin Ironworks and Mitsubishi Kogyo Cheongjin Ironworks. Some of it also went to the Anshan and Benxi Lake ironworks in Manchuria, and the Yawata, Hirohata, and Wanishi ironworks in Japan, but not in large amounts. Even so, the powder ore supplied by the Musan mine for use in sintering played an important role at the Yawata and Hirohata ironworks in 1943 and 1944.

Iron Sulfide

Ube Chisso Kogyo, a fertilizer manufacturer affiliated with Ube Cement, purchased the Dancheon mine located in the eastern part of northern Korea (Hamgyeongnam-do) in 1936 and operated it until the end of the war. It was one of the most prominent mines in Korea where superior iron sulfide could be found. Because it was located deep in the mountains at an elevation of 1,000 meters, the Ube headquarters invested vast sums to build a road and install a 15-kilometer aerial cableway. The mined ore was shipped to Ube in Japan and used as a source of sulfuric acid. Because marine shipping became difficult near the end of the war, all of the mined ore during that period was sent to Heungnam Fertilizer Plant in Korea.

In addition, Nippon Kogyo operated rich iron sulfide mines (the Geumhwa and Wonbuk mines) in the eastern part of northern Korea (the northern part of Gangwon-do). By 1944, a total of 45,000 tons had been mined there.

Lead and Zinc

Rich lead and zinc mines included the Geomdeok mine in the eastern part of northern Korea (Dancheon-gun, Hamgyeongnam-do), the Seongcheon mine in the western part of northern Korea, and the Eunbong mine. These were owned respectively by Nippon Kogyo, Sansei Kogyo (belonging to the Mitsui Kozan group), and Chugai Kogyo (belonging to the Nippon Kayaku group). In 1944, the Geomdeok mine produced about 3,000 tons of lead ore and 10,000 tons of zinc ore; the Seongcheon mine produced about 1,000 tons of lead ore and 6,000 tons of zinc ore.

Magnesite:
A Resource for Fireproof Bricks and Metallic Magnesium

In 1939, the Government-General ordered the establishment of Chosen Magnesite Kaihatsu Kabushiki Kaisha as a *kokusaku-kaisha*, or semi-state company. The Government-General and Toyo Takushoku were the major investors, and capitalization was 15 million yen. As an investment in kind, the Government-General provided the company with the Yongyang magnesite mine located in Dancheon-gun, Hamgyeongnam-do, in the eastern part of northern Korea. In addition, Nippon Seitetsu, Mitsubishi Kogyo, Shinagawa Shirorenga, Nippon Magnesite Kagaku Kogyo, Kobe Seikosho, Tokyo Shibaura Denki, Asahi Denka Kogyo, and other companies that needed magnesite ore invested in the new company.

The Yongyang mine was estimated to have about 100 million tons of ore reserves, but it was left undeveloped for many years because it was located in an inaccessible hinterland. Chosen Magnesite Kaihatsu invested 22 million yen by the end of 1942 to construct a railroad for the exclusive use of the mine and began its development. By September of that year, 80 percent of the infrastructure for the mine had been completed.

Barium: Used in the Chemical Industry

The richest barium mine was the Changdo mine located in the eastern part of northern Korea (Gimhwa-gun, Gangwon-do). The barite mined there was known for its world-class quality, with a barium sulfate content of 95 percent. The Changdo mine accounted for half of all barite mined in Korea. The mine's owner was Nakagawa Kogyo founded by Nakagawa Minato, who was born in Fukuoka Prefecture in 1878. The company chemically processed the barite to produce barium nitrate and barium chloride, materials necessary for the manufacture of explosives, dyes, and other products.

Zircon, Tungsten, Molybdenum, Beryllium, and Strontium: Used in Special Steel Materials and Chemicals in Weapons

In 1943, Nippon Zirconium Kabushiki Kaisha was founded in Seoul. Although it was a small company capitalized at 100,000 yen, it played an important role in the development of zircon mines in northern Korea. Zircon was found widely in heavy sand (discussed below). At the direction of the Japanese military, Nippon Zirconium received capital and technology from Tokyo-based Nippon Seiko and the Kiyu Kinzoku Seiren Kenkyusho (Rare Metal Refinery Research Institute).

There was almost no tungsten ore in Japan, but large deposits existed in Korea. Of these, the Baengnyeon mine in the western part of northern Korea (Hwanghae-do) was known as the richest. With a deposit 2.5 kilometers long, it was much larger than any other mine of the same type in Korea. It was purchased in 1937 by Kobayashi Kogyo, a company based in Korea, which also owned the Sangdong mine in the northern part of southern Korea (Gangwon-do). Beginning in 1940, at the direction of the government, Kobayashi Kogyo worked to boost production of tungsten ore. Its share of tungsten ore output in the Japanese Empire reached 75 percent, and the company owner, Kobayashi Uneo (see Column 3), became known as the "Tungsten King of the Peninsula." In addition to Kobayashi Kogyo, Nippon Kogyo extracted tungsten ore from the Giju mine in the western part of northern Korea (Hwanghae-do). In 1943, the Giju mine employed 1,600 workers and produced 1,900 tons of tungsten ore with a quality grade of 69 percent.

There were plentiful deposits of wulfenite, an ore that contains molybdenum, in the eastern part of northern Korea (the northern part of Gangwon-do) and in the western part of southern Korea (Jeollabuk-do). During the war, the wulfenite mines were operated by the semi-state company Chosen Kogyo Shinko Kabushiki Kaisha (founded in 1940 with a capitalization of 10 million yen), Showa Denko, Nihon Koshuha Jukogyo, and other companies.

The previously mentioned Nakagawa Kogyo also mined beryl at the Changdo mine. From this, the company extracted strontium (a metal alloy material) and beryllium (a constituent of luminous paint).

Silica Sand: A Raw Material for Glass
Japan itself did not have many sources of silica sand, but there were large-scale producing areas on the western side of the Korean Peninsula. Near the end of the war, imports of silica sand were cut off from Indochina, increasing the importance of Korean silica sand. Tokai Kogyo, a subsidiary of Asahi Glass (merged to become Mitsubishi Kasei in 1944), began operating in Korea in 1914 and produced 72,000 tons of silica sand in 1942, 61,000 tons in 1943, and 40,000 tons in 1944.

Graphite, Mica, Fluorite, and Apatite:
Various Kinds of Industrial Materials
Toho Kogyo got its start in 1934 and began operating graphite mines in the western part of northern Korea (Ganggye-gun and Guseong-gun in Pyeonganbuk-do). Toho Kogyo was the largest producer of vein graph-

ite in the Japanese Empire, with a 90 percent share of the market. In 1944, it produced 7,000 tons of graphite for use in electrodes.

Chosen Unmo Kaihatsu Hanbai Kabushiki Kaisha developed mica for electrical and heat insulation applications. After its founding in 1939, with financing received from mainstream Japanese electric appliance manufacturers such as Tokyo Shibaura Denki, Hitachi Seisakusho, Fuji Denki, and Mitsubishi Denki, the company operated mica mines and factories throughout northern Korea. The Government-General designated Chosen Unmo Kaihatsu Hanbai as a *tosei kaisha* (state-controlled company) for mica development. Electrified equipment was installed in all of its mines, and in 1944, it met its government-mandated output quota of 100 tons of mica.

Fluorite, a source of fluorine, could be found in the excellent Mulgae mine (Hwanghae-do) operated by Sumitomo Kogyo in the eastern part of northern Korea. The fluorite produced by this mine was supplied to light metal factories in Korea for use in the aluminum industry. In 1944, the Mulgae mine produced 15,000 tons of fluorite.

In 1939, a large deposit (tens of millions of tons) of apatite was discovered in Dancheon-gun, Hamgyeongnam-do, in the eastern part of northern Korea. The ore had an apatite content of 20 to 50 percent (equivalent to 10 to 20 percent phosphoric acid). To develop this resource, Chosen Rinko Kabushiki Kaisha was founded in 1940. The company operated several other apatite mines in northern Korea, as well. The mined ore was an important raw material for phosphorus fertilizer and was supplied to Heungnam Fertilizer Plant and other chemical plants in Korea.

Uranium: Nuclear Fuel

Korea had deposits of monazite (composed principally of phosphorus, cerium, and thorium compounds). Monazite also contains compounds of uranium and other elements. In 1940, the Imperial Japanese Army recognized the significance of manufacturing an atomic bomb. The next year it entrusted research on this project to Dr. Nishina Yoshio of the

Institute of Physical and Chemical Research (RIKEN), a private-sector research facility. Nishina set his sights on Korean monazite as the source ore for uranium. Research on Korean monazite had already been conducted as early as 1918 by Professor Nakamura Shintaro of Kyoto Imperial University. In the 1930s, Dr. Iimori Satoyasu of RIKEN published detailed research on the subject.

Generally, monazite is a black, sandy ore that contains such ores as magnetite, ilmenite, spinel, and tourmaline. This is why it is called "black sand." However, when it contains garnet, monazite has a reddish-brown hue, prompting Iimori and others to call it "heavy sand." Monazite sandy ore is distributed in the gold diggings located in the western part of northern Korea. The heavy sand on the banks of the Daedong and Cheongcheon rivers was particularly rich in monazite, as high as 3 to 4 percent. The monazite in one area between the two rivers (located in Pyeongwon-gun, Pyeongannam-do) contained 9 percent thorium and 0.1 percent uranium.

Northern Korea also produced ores that contained large quantities of uranium (uranium 238 and 235), as well as fergusonite, autunite, and torbernite. In most cases, these ores were found mixed with monazite and columbite (the source ore for tantalum and niobium) in pegmatite. Fergusonite was produced along with heavy sand at the Gukgeun mine in Yeonbaek-gun, Hwanghae-do, in the western part of northern Korea. (Although located just south of the 38th parallel, the mine became part of North Korean territory after the Korean War.) This was a high-quality sandy ore, containing as much as 8.4 percent uranium. Autunite and torbernite were mined at the Eungok mine (Sakju-gun, Pyeonganbuk-do) and the Dannok mine (Cheolwon-gun, Gangwon-do).

Chosen Kogyo Kaihatsu, founded by Noguchi Shitagau, was renamed Nicchitsu Kogyo Kaihatsu in 1939 and followed government directives to develop rare metal mines. In 1943, Nicchitsu Kogyo Kaihatsu Seonam Mining Station, which was located in the western part of northern Korea (Cheolsan-gun, Pyeonganbuk-do), began excavating heavy sand. Through simple sorting, they obtained ore with a monazite content of

50 percent, which was delivered to a smelting works in Heungnam (discussed below). At the smelting works, the static electricity method developed by Nippon Chisso's electrical technology division was used to refine the ore to a content ratio exceeding 95 percent. The facility could produce one ton of refined ore per day, and it also obtained ilmenite and garnet as by-products. The cerium extracted from the monazite became an important raw material for the manufacture of carbon rods at the carbon factory in Heungnam.

The Imperial Japanese Army began extracting fergusonite at the Gukgeun mine in June 1944. The plan was to obtain half (500 kilograms) of the uranium 235 needed to manufacture an atomic bomb (the other half was to be mined in Ishikawa-cho, Fukushima Prefecture, in Japan). In June 1945, however, the Army abandoned its plan to manufacture an atomic bomb because of technical problems (the Imperial Japanese Navy pursued development of atomic bombs separately, but that project was cancelled as well).

Industry: Maximizing Production to Meet Military Demand

From the end of the 1930s, production in Korea expanded in many fields related to the military, including ironmaking, metallurgy, light metals, chemicals, and textiles. This trend was the result of investments made by companies in Korea, especially those connected to Noguchi Shitagau, and major zaibatsu conglomerates in Japan, such as Mitsui, Mitsubishi, and Sumitomo. A secret factory that manufactured rocket fuel for the Imperial Japanese Navy was one new facility built as part of this trend (see pp.158–159). Near the end of the war, other many companies in Japan constructed factories in Korea in compliance with orders from the military.

In the following section, I examine how production increased in the heavy and chemical industries.

Ironmaking

Ironmaking facilities were expanded at Nippon Seitetsu Gyeomipo Ironworks and Nihon Koshuha Jukogyo Seongjin Plant, and new ironworks were also constructed, including Nippon Seitetsu Cheongjin Ironworks, Mitsubishi Kogyo Cheongjin Ironworks, and Mitsubishi Seiko Pyongyang Ironworks.

A preparatory smelting furnace was completed at Nippon Seitetsu Gyeomipo Ironworks in 1940, which in combination with an improved furnace type, greatly boosted the production capacity of steel. Construction of a low-phosphorus pig iron furnace was also pursued, with most of the pig iron (a raw material for special steel) delivered to the Kure Naval Arsenal in Japan. This furnace, which featured a special design invented in 1922 by Japanese researchers, made it possible to remove phosphorus and sulfur from the injected iron ore regardless of how much phosphorus the ore contained. Many difficulties were encountered in operating the furnace, but efficiency was increased through improvements made to the cooling plates and bricks. In 1943–44, ten specially made small-scale smelting furnaces with 20-ton capacities (for a total annual production capacity of 50,000 tons) were built by order of the Japanese government. All ten furnaces were operated, but technical problems resulted in poor product quality and unreliable production. The amount of steel ingots produced annually reached its peak in 1942 and subsequently declined, but production stayed at the 100,000-ton level until 1944.

In 1944, the Japanese government ordered the transfer of a steel sheet rolling mill to Gyeomipo Ironworks from Amagasaki Seitetsu in Japan. By the end of the war, Gyeomipo Ironworks had increased its production capacity to 350,000 tons of pig iron and 150,000 tons of steel, and its steel rolling capacity had increased to 170,000 tons. This was still very low, however, compared with Nippon Seitetsu's steelmaking facilities in Japan, which had a total production capacity of 4.5 million tons of pig iron and 4.2 million tons of steel.

After its founding, Nihon Koshuha Jukogyo grew largely because of a sharp increase in military demand for special steel that few companies in Japan could supply. In 1938–39, the company increased its capitalization to 40 million yen to expand Seongjin Plant. Its main product was high speed steel manufactured using in-house ferro-tungsten. In 1940, the total ferro-tungsten output of the Japanese Empire was 4,373 tons, of which 1,562 tons was produced by Nihon Koshuha. Most of that amount was manufactured at Seongjin Plant.

Seongjin Plant also manufactured large quantities of carbon tool steel, special tool steel, and cutting tools. In 1940, it began making bearing steel (chrome steel). Before then, Japan imported most of its bearing steel, but importation became difficult after the outbreak of World War II. In response, the Japanese government set its sights on promoting the complete domestic production of bearing steel and bearings, and it decided to subsidize domestic special steel manufacturers. Nihon Koshuha began manufacturing bearing steel with support from those subsidies. It is unclear where that steel was mainly delivered, but after 1940, the likely recipients were arsenals in Japan and weapons plants (discussed below) in southern Korea. In 1938, Seongjin Plant was placed under the supervision of the Army Arsenal. The head office itself was designated as a munitions company in 1944 under the Munitions Companies Act. Near the end of the war, production directives from the military increased for steel used to make guns and rifles, occupying third highest production target after high speed tool steel and bearing steel. Seongjin Plant drastically increased its production of steel for guns and rifles and received commendations from the Government-General and the Japanese garrison force in Korea in 1945.

Construction of Nippon Seitetsu's large-scale Cheongjin Ironworks (Seishin Seitetsujo) began in April 1939. The Government-General and the Japanese garrison force in Korea had long urged Nippon Seitetsu to construct the ironworks and, in preparation, had reinforced or newly constructed breakwaters at Cheongjin Port, secured ships for transporting materials, purchased land for the building site, and otherwise facilitated the project.

Plans called for iron ore to be procured from Musan, and coking coal from the Mishan and Hegang coal mines in eastern Manchuria. These materials were to be used to create a fully integrated production system, ranging from pig iron to finished steel. Nippon Seitetsu invested in the project, and various related companies and plants were established in quick succession, including Chosen Magnesite, Hokusen Takushoku Tetsudo, Mosan Tekko Kaihatsu, Nihon Rozai Seizo Cheongjin Plant, and Mitsuzan Tanko. However, construction of Cheongjin Ironworks was greatly delayed because of shortages of materials and labor, bitter cold, and bad weather. Initial plans called for two smelting furnaces to begin operating simultaneously, but these plans were changed so that efforts could be focused on getting just the first smelting furnace up and running. As a result, the first smelting furnace was finally ignited three years later in May 1942, with a pig iron production capacity of 175,000 tons. The plant also brought its own power generation facility online at that time, powered by exhaust gas from the furnace. Construction of the second smelting furnace continued at top speed (called the "Fireball Movement"), resulting in it coming online in December 1942.

About 80 percent of the iron ore processed by Cheongjin Ironworks came from the Musan iron mine, with the remaining 20 percent from other Korean mines. In 1943–44, a small smelting furnace was installed and attempts were made to fire it using anthracite, but the results were unsatisfactory. In March 1945, the decision was made to transfer small and medium-sized steelmaking and rolling facilities to Cheongjin Ironworks from Osaka, as well as a 400-ton metal mixer from Yawata. However, the war ended after most of the basic construction had been completed but before the equipment transfer took place. In fiscal year 1944, Cheongjin Ironworks produced 226,683 tons of pig iron.

Cheongjin Ironworks of Mitsubishi Kogyo, a mining company, was a medium-sized facility. In 1937, Mitsubishi Kogyo teamed up with Manchuria-based Showa Seikosho (Showa Ironworks) to purchase patent rights for a direct steelmaking method using a rotary kiln from the famous German steelmaker Krupp. This was a special technology that converted iron ore into steel using a direct reduction method. The following year, Mitsubishi Kogyo began constructing its ironworks, which would employ this technology. Raw materials included iron ore from Musan and anthracite from the western part of northern Korea; the first furnace was ignited in 1939. By 1943, six furnaces were in operation, and two electric furnaces were being used to produce carbon steel. In 1942, the facility produced 56,000 tons of steel. It maintained annual production at the 50,000-ton level from then until the end of the war.

Mitsubishi Seiko Pyongyang Ironworks was a large-scale, integrated steelmaking facility located in Gangseon on the banks of the Daedong River. Construction was planned by Mitsubishi Juko (Mitsubishi Heavy Industry) in 1940, and its purpose was to increase production of special steel using self-supplied steelmaking resources and electric furnaces. Gangseon was selected as the site for the facility because of its proximity to electric power generated on the Yalu River and to iron ore. Initial construction costs climbed to 16 million yen, which was procured by the Mitsubishi zaibatsu conglomerate. In 1942, the steelmaking division of Mitsubishi Juko merged with Mitsubishi Kozai to create Mitsubishi Seiko, capitalized at 30 million yen. The new company took over the operations of Mitsubishi Juko's ironworks facilities in Nagasaki and Pyongyang.

After responsibility for construction of Pyongyang Ironworks was transferred to Mitsubishi Seiko, work was greatly delayed because of a shortage of materials. Nevertheless, the facility was nearly completed by the end of 1943, when operations were initiated with 629 employees. Plans called for producing carbon steel and ferroalloys through a direct steelmaking method using an electric furnace; products were then to be supplied to the Imperial Japanese Army and Navy. However, because the direct steelmaking method presented many technical and financial challenges, the reduced iron method was used instead. Later, this method also presented problems, so that ultimately the facility made steel through a converter steelmaking method using cupola furnaces. The Imperial Japanese Army issued many orders for increased production of steel products in general and bullet-proof steel plates in particular. In response, Pyongyang Ironworks proposed a massive expansion of its facilities, introducing a large steel plate rolling mill. But construction proved difficult and only less than half of the project was completed by the end of the war. Although steel was produced at the facility, none of it was ever delivered.

In addition to the facilities discussed above, three other ironworks were constructed: Chosen Seitetsu Pyongyang Ironworks, Nippon Gen-

Table 4-5.

Facilities Operated by Chosen Seitetsu, Nippon Gentetsu, and Nippon Kokan

Plant name	Summary
Chosen Seitetsu Pyongyang Ironworks	Chosen Seitetsu (capitalized at 60 million yen) was founded in 1941 by Daido Seiko and Toyo Takushoku. This facility was a large-scale pig iron plant using electric furnaces with a planned annual production capacity of 300,000 tons of pig iron, as well as 200,000 tons of cast steel, hollow drill steel, bullet steel, and ferroalloys. In 1943, a smelting furnace was completed and bullet steel was produced under military order. The war ended before full production was achieved.
Nippon Gentetsu Cheongjin Plant	In 1943, in accordance with emergency orders issued by the Imperial Japanese Army on the basis of the Fiscal 1943 Imperial Japanese Army Guidelines for Special Increased Production of Iron and Steel, Nihon Koshuha Jukogyo founded Nippon Gentetsu (capitalized at 10 million yen). Plans called for an annual production of 30,000 tons of iron using the low-frequency electric method. The Army facilitated the procurement of financing and materials and the purchase of the land. Construction began in August 1943, and the furnace was ignited in December of that year, with an annual production capacity of 30,000 tons. In January 1944, the plant was placed under the supervision of the Army's Incheon Arsenal. In 1944, it produced 11,492 tons of raw iron (granular iron produced through electric furnace smelting).
Nippon Kokan Wonsan Ironworks	In 1943, Nippon Kokan planned the construction of ten 20-ton smelting furnaces. In May 1944, the first furnace was completed. It operated smoothly and achieved superior results compared with other small-scale smelting furnaces operating in Korea at the time. Beginning in February 1945, it became impossible to continue operations because shipments of coking coal from northern China had been cut off.

Source: Kimura and Abe 2003, 32–33.

tetsu Cheongjin Plant, and Nippon Kokan Wonsan Ironworks. Summaries of these plants are provided in table 4-5.

Smelting Nonferrous Metals

In the nonferrous metal sector, facilities were expanded at both Nippon Kogyo Jinnampo Smelting Works and the smelting works in Heungnam.

In 1941, Nippon Kogyo installed new zinc electrolysis equipment at the Jinnampo Smelting Works with a production capacity of 500 tons per month. Including temporary workers, the facility employed more than 4,600 workers at the time. This was comparable to the number of employees at Nippon Kogyo's main smelting facilities in Hitachi and Saganoseki in Japan.

In 1937–41, Jinnampo Smelting Works had an average copper smelting capacity of 218,286 tons per year (in terms of the amount of ore processed), which was equivalent to about 40 percent of that of the smelting works in Hitachi. No significant decrease in the amount of ore processed occurred in later years (230,000 tons in 1942, 180,000 tons in 1944). In 1943, the company began construction of a plant to produce sulfuric acid and alumina, as well as a cryolite plant (for the manufacture of aluminum fluoride and aluminum hydroxide). By the end of the war, these plants were 50 percent and 80 percent completed, respectively. Beginning in March 1944, Nippon Kogyo began smelting tungsten ore extracted from its Giju mine (mentioned earlier) to produce ferro-tungsten. It produced a total of 452 tons by the end of the war.

In Heungnam, Chosen Kogyo Kaihatsu constructed a smelting works next to the fertilizer plant in 1933. Using the facilities and technologies of the fertilizer plant, the company smelted the ore extracted from its own mines. After construction, the smelting works was continually expanded. In 1941, it reached annual smelting capacities of 2.7 tons of gold, 40 tons of silver, 3,200 tons of copper, and 4,800 tons of lead. Zinc electrolysis equipment was also installed. The company achieved many technical innovations, including the use of electrolytic oxygen in smelting furnaces for the electrolysis of copper. In addition, the company installed flotation sorting equipment for the re-sorting of low-grade Korean ore. This equipment improved the recovery of gold, silver, copper, lead, zinc, and iron sulfide and enhanced smelting capacity. It also made it possible to sort fluorite for aluminum and lead smelting, as well as to sort monazite, titanium ore, garnet, and columbite. In 1943, Chosen Kogyo Kaihatsu began smelting nickel using copper smelting facilities. In July 1945, the company started constructing a nickel electrolysis plant, but the war ended before it could be completed.

Other smelting plants included Sumitomo Kogyo Wonsan Smelting Works (built in 1937) and Sansei Kogyo Yongampo Smelting Works (built in 1941). These, along with Nippon Kogyo Jinnampo Smelting Works, were called Korea's "big three" gold smelting facilities. Sansei Kogyo Yongampo Smelting Works was built by Mitsui Kozan in the suburbs of Sinuiju in the northwestern part of northern Korea. This was done at the order of the Government-General, which was promoting gold production. The facility smelted gold, silver, copper, lead, and zinc, but the copper smelting operation was transferred to the Mankayan mine in the Philippines by order of the Imperial Japanese Army in September 1943.

Light Metals

Aluminum and magnesium are the two major light metals. Because their manufacture generally entails complicated chemical processing, plants that produce them have characteristics similar to chemical plants.

To make aluminum, alumina must be extracted from raw ore and subjected to electrolysis. Since the nineteenth century, the most common way to extract alumina was to treat bauxite with caustic soda. Two other methods, the ammonium sulfate method and the soda lime method, were developed before the war started, and each one uses alunite or alumina shale. In Japan in the 1920s, Tokyo Industrial Research Institute and RIKEN researched the manufacture of aluminum using alumina shale from Manchuria and bauxite. This work began to be commercialized in the 1930s. In Korea, the Government-General's Fuels and

Refining Research Center and Chosen Chisso began researching the manufacture of aluminum around 1930, using alumina shale extracted in Pyongyang or Manchuria.

The raw material for making magnesium is either magnesite or bittern (magnesium chloride). Magnesium production in Japan was promoted by RIKEN in the 1930s, based on research for processing magnesite from Manchuria and domestic bittern. At about the same time, Chosen Chisso began producing magnesium from magnesite and bittern from northern Korea.

After 1937, demand for fuselages and parts used in military aircraft increased greatly. Therefore, programs were launched to increase production of aluminum and magnesium using locally generated electrical power and local ores in northern Korea, Manchuria, and northern China. The Government-General promulgated the Korea Light Metal Production Undertaking Order in 1939, and in 1940 it ordered Chosen Chisso to research the manufacture of aluminum. From 1942, the Emergency Plan for Drastic Increases in Production of Light Metals was implemented in northern Korea to help continue the war against the United States. Construction began on large manufacturing plants throughout the region, with a targeted total production capacity of 200,000 tons of aluminum and 20,000 tons of magnesium by 1945. However, resource shortages and technical flaws impeded the construction and operation of each plant. Summaries of the major light metal plants are presented in table 4-6.

Weapons, Ships, Machinery, and Castings

In this sector, existing plants were expanded and new plants were constructed in rapid succession. New construction was more evident in southern Korea than in the north.

The number of employees at Pyongyang Munitions Plant was increased to 2,000 by 1938. To guard against American attacks, the Imperial Japanese Army pursued a program of moving production facilities underground. Inmates in Pyongyang Prison were mobilized to construct a huge underground plant in the rocky mountains about ten kilometers from Pyongyang. Construction was nearly completed by the end of the war, and one member of a medical team that visited the site later testified that he was overwhelmed by its scale. Just before the end of the war, the main products manufactured at this plant were bullets and bombs, with a bullet production capacity of 180,000 per month. At the time

Table 4-6.

Light Metal Plants

Plant name	Summary
Nippon Chisso Heungnam Aluminum Plant	Founded in 1937. Initially using alunite from southern Korea and later alumina shale from northern China, it succeeded in making aluminum products that were over 99.5 percent pure from low-grade alumina. It failed to maintain steady product quality or increase production.
Chosen Keikinzoku Jinnampo Plant	In 1938, RIKEN founded Chosen Riken Kinzoku (capitalized at 15 million yen). The new company entered the Showa Denko group in 1942 and was renamed Chosen Keikinzoku in 1944. The plan was to build an integrated production system that would produce alumina and aluminum from alumina shale procured from the Pyongyang area. Construction began in 1939 and aluminum production began the next year. In 1941, construction began on a magnesium plant, which was completed in 1944. At the end of 1942, part of an alumina electrolytic cell was converted for use in an expanded magnesium production system. The aluminum division became fully operational in 1943 and increased production. The facility was being expanded when the war ended.
Chosen Shinko Kinzoku Sinuiju Plant	In 1939, Kobe Seikosho, Dai-Nippon Engyo, Taiyo Sangyo, and others founded Toyo Kinzoku with a capitalization of 50 million yen. The company was renamed Chosen Shinko Kinzoku in 1942. Plans called for annual production of 1,000 tons of magnesium using a combined bittern/ore method. Operation began in 1941. Because of a shortage of bittern, only half of the electrolytic furnaces were used. The plant produced 260 tons of magnesium in 1943, 452 tons in 1944, and 127 tons in the first quarter of 1945 (the production quota was 126 tons).

the war ended, the plant employed 6,000 workers (of whom 5,000 were Korean).

In 1940, the Army established an arsenal and built a factory and a training center for engineers in Incheon. The factory manufactured bayonets, rifles, and bombs. Its production capacity in 1943–45 was 10,000 bayonets, 9,000 rifles, and 4,800 small and medium-sized bombs per

Plant name	Summary
Asahi Keikinzoku Giyang Plant	In November 1943, under the orders of the military, the Government-General, the Light Metals Control Association (Keikinzoku Tosei Kai), and the Ministry of Commerce and Industries, Nippon Keikinzoku established Asahi Keikinzoku with a capitalization of 40 million yen. Plans called for the construction of the largest magnesium plant in Asia, with an annual production capacity of 5,000 tons and located midway between Pyongyang and Jinnampo. The raw material was to be magnesite, and electric power was to be procured from the Supung Power Station. At the end of 1944, part of the first phase of the construction plan was completed, and electrification of 36 electrolytic cells was initiated in January 1945. The boiler remained unfinished and a series of breakdowns prevented the plant from achieving good production results. It only produced 37 tons of metallic magnesium by the end of the war, at which time the second construction phase had been undertaken to build the first bomb-proof underground plant in Korea.
Chosen Denko Jinnampo Plant	Under military orders, Showa Denko founded Chosen Denko in 1943 with a capitalization of 100 million yen. Funding was provided by the Wartime Financial Corporation in Japan. Plans called for the construction of an aluminum plant with an annual production capacity of 50,000 tons, using electrical power from the Supung and Ganggye power stations, and alumina shale from northern China. A shortage of materials and the military drafting of personnel made construction work difficult. At the end of the war, only a power plant building and generator, 20 electrolytic cells, and three mercury rectifiers had been constructed or installed.

Source: Kimura and Abe 2003, 38–43.

month. It is estimated that the facility employed several thousand workers at the time the war ended.

Large, privately owned factories included Mitsubishi Seiko Incheon Plant, Chosen Kikai Seisakusho Incheon Plant, and Chosen Jukogyo Busan Shipyard. Mitsubishi Seiko originally purchased its Incheon plant from Hironaka Shoko (a company that manufactured and sold machinery) in 1942. This had been a machine manufacturing plant, and after the purchase, its facilities were expanded and it began manufacturing special steel plate, mortars, and fabricated parts for weapons under order from the Army. At the end of the war, the facility employed 1,230 workers.

Chosen Kikai Seisakusho was a subsidiary of Yokoyama Kogyo, a Tokyo-based boiler manufacturer. In 1937 the company built a plant in Incheon that manufactured steel bars, boilers for naval vessels, mining machinery, and various kinds of weapons. Near the end of the war, the company formulated a plan to produce large quantities of submarines to be used by the Army for transport and began constructing a specialized dock for that purpose. At the end of the war, the facility employed more than 5,000 workers. Chosen Jukogyo was established in 1937 by investors that included Toyo Takushoku, Mitsubishi Juko, and Chosen Shokusan Ginko (Korea Industrial Bank). In Busan, it constructed the largest shipyard in Korea, which employed 2,800 workers at the time the war ended.

In addition, the following companies in Japan established plants manufacturing military-related equipment in the Seoul/Incheon region beginning in the late 1930s: Mitsubishi Denki, Showa Seiko, Yuasa Chikudenchi, Koyo Seiko, Nippon Seiko, Nippon Sharyo Seizo, Hitachi Seisakusho, Tokyo Shibaura Denki, Oki Denki, and Matsushita Denki. As a result, the machinery industry expanded quickly in southern Korea, following the textile industry, which was already well established.

Chemicals: Rocket Fuel

In the chemical industry, one factory specialized in the manufacture of rocket fuel: Nicchitsu Nenryo Kogyo Yongheung Plant. Nicchitsu Nenryo Kogyo was a wholly owned subsidiary of the Nicchitsu Conglomerate and was founded in 1941 with a capitalization of 30 million yen. Yongheung Plant was located in Heungnam, where construction began in 1938. The goal was to manufacture iso-octane, a liquid fuel with a high-octane rating, by order of the Imperial Japanese Navy. This was a top-secret facility called the NZ Plant (NZ was a code name for rocket fuel; the "N" stood for Nippon Chisso or Navy, and the "Z" for the Z flag [meaning the final battle]). To the extent possible, technology, materials, and equipment that were available in Heungnam were mobilized to construct the plant.

The first construction phase was essentially completed in 1941, leading to the successful synthesis of iso-octane through the processing of acetylene, acetaldehyde, and butanol from carbide. The plant began operating in June 1942, but a series of equipment breakdowns limited the operation rate to about 50 percent. The second construction phase began in 1940 and brought the plant close to completion in the summer of 1944. However, at the direct order of top Navy brass, construction plans were changed to focus on the manufacture of *Rogo-otsuyaku* rocket fuel.

Rogo-otsuyaku was used to power the German rocket-powered Messerschmitt Me 163 Komet and V2 rocket (the "Ro" in the name stands for "rocket"). As is well-known among Japanese war historians, a lieutenant colonel of technology from the Imperial Japanese Navy boarded a Japanese submarine (*I-go*) and then a transport plane to bring basic information back to Japan in the summer of 1944. The Navy's plan was to snatch victory from the jaws of defeat by developing a rocket-propelled interceptor plane (called Shusui) that could collide with American B-29 bombers (a suicide fighter, *tokkoki*). It was to be fueled with *Rogo-otsuyaku*. More than twenty chemical companies, including Nippon Chisso, Mitsubishi Kasei, and Nissan Kagaku, were ordered to manufacture the fuel.

Initially there were three fuel varieties (A, B, and C), to which a fourth variety (D) was later added. Yongheung Plant was to manufacture

Type A (an aqueous solution of 80 percent hydrogen peroxide) and Type B (80 percent hydrazine). The plant was to produce more of these liquids than any other company. The construction of the hydrazine plant proceeded at an extraordinarily fast pace, being completed in just one month. Except for reference to documents from the German military for part of the facility, the design was conceived and executed by the Japanese themselves. At the end of 1944, just when hydrazine production got on track, the Navy suddenly ordered it to be halted. The fuel production program had suffered a serious setback because necessary materials other than hydrazine could not be procured. Nippon Chisso was completely inexperienced in the manufacture of hydrogen peroxide and was struggling, although by the end of the war they had delivered at least 50 cubic meters to the Navy. In the spring of 1945, plans were made to dig a tunnel under a nearby mountain and move the plant inside, but the war ended before the plans could be implemented.

The manufacture of rocket fuel was also planned for Dai-Nippon Boseki Cheongjin Plant. In 1937, the company had decided to operate in Korea and began constructing a rayon factory in Cheongjin. At the time, the Japanese government was against expanding non-military production such as textiles in Japan. But the Government-General, actively supporting the construction of a rayon plant in Korea, decided that rayon production would be divided between Dai-Nippon Boseki Cheongjin Rayon Plant (primarily long-fiber rayon) and Kanegafuchi Kogyo Pyongyang Rayon/Staple Fiber Plant (primarily short-fiber rayon). The first phase of construction for the Cheongjin plant was completed in February 1941; the 99-hectare site included a sulfuric acid/rayon plant, a sodium sulfide plant, a pharmaceutical plant, and an in-house power generator. The plant had a rayon production capacity of 8,700 tons per year, about the same as a medium-sized plant in Japan. It was enough to easily satisfy demand for rayon in Korea.

In August 1944 Cheongjin Rayon Plant was renamed Cheongjin Chemical Plant, and in April 1945, it was designated as a munitions company. Meanwhile, progress was made on constructing facilities in the plant for the manufacture of aluminum fluoride, a necessary auxiliary agent for the electrolytic process used to make aluminum. In accordance with Navy orders, preparations also were made to manufacture Type A rocket fuel. Half of the plant's facilities were to be dedicated to this project, with rushed construction work beginning in May 1945. However, the war ended before production could begin.

Chemicals: Gunpowder

Gunpowder plants grew quickly as well. For public safety reasons, the Ordinance for the Control of Firearms and Gunpowder prohibited the manufacture of gunpowder in Korea until 1934. After the ordinance was revised, demand for gunpowder burgeoned in tandem with the development of the mining and manufacturing industries, and the manufacture of gunpowder in northern Korea became quite active, based on the development of the chloro-alkali electrolysis, ammonia, and fats and oils industries. The Government-General established the Gunpowder Committee in 1939 and the Blasting Research Center in 1940, with the aim of researching gunpowder and increasing its production in Korea. By 1941, Korea had become self-sufficient in its gunpowder supply.

The largest gunpowder factory in Korea was Chosen Chisso Kayaku Heungnam Plant. In 1935, Nippon Chisso established Chosen Chisso Kayaku with a capitalization of 20 million yen and built a plant near its fertilizer plant in Heungnam. At its peak, the facility employed 2,500 workers.

At the ammonium nitrate plant of Chosen Chisso Kayaku, the basic raw materials—ammonia and oxygen—were piped in from the fertilizer plant and processed in fifteen concentrating columns to make nitric acid. This plant had the largest nitric acid production capacity of any facility in the Japanese Empire. The black gunpowder plant manufactured gunpowder for fuses, explosives for mining applications, and products for use by hunters and the Imperial Japanese Army. From 1938 to 1944, plant production of black gunpowder for the Army increased from 200 tons to 600 tons. The guncotton plant procured cotton linters from the cotton-growing regions in southern Korea and installed the only integrated production system for guncotton in the Japanese Empire. The carlit plant manufactured explosives for mining and civil engineering use.

Other large-scale, mechanized facilities constructed by Chosen Chisso Kayaku included a detonator plant, a fuse plant, and a dynamite plant. The detonator plant was completed in 1939. To conserve mercury (used as a raw material), the plant manufactured detonators using lead nitride. The technology was originally developed in the United States, but Japan was the first to use it on an industrial scale. All of the raw materials for lead nitride, including hydrazine, alcohol nitrite, and caustic soda, were procured from various plants in Heungnam. In 1944, a decision was made to convert the fourth dynamite plant so that it could manufacture smokeless gunpowder for military use. Construction of the facility was nearly complete at the end of the war, but it never shipped any products. In August 1944, the Imperial Japanese Navy ordered the expansion of the Carlit Explosives Plant and set annual production targets for K2 and K3 explosives (used in depth charges) at 1,500 tons. The military-use "SU gunpowder" plant manufactured hexogen high explosives from urotropine produced by Yeongan Plant. Overall production fell substantially in early 1945, however, because of a shortage of raw materials and the military drafting of employees.

In addition, Nippon Kayaku established a subsidiary in Korea in 1935 and built a plant in Haeju in the western part of northern Korea. This was followed by Asano Cement in 1938 and Nippon Yushi in 1940, which produced various explosives, detonators, and dynamite (the Chosen Asano Carlit Bongsan Plant in the western part of northern Korea and the Chosen Yushi Incheon Plant).

Chemicals: Optical Weapons and Other Chemicals

Plans were pursued to construct plants in the optical weapons field. In 1921, Dai-Nippon Seito built a plant in Pyongyang to process sugar beets grown in Korea. During the war, many sugar-producing and -refining plants in Japan either had their operations curtailed or were shut down as a result of plant conversions to meet military demand. Dai-Nippon Seito Pyongyang Plant met the same fate. In July 1943, Hitachi Seisakusho bought this plant and renovated it as a munitions plant. The company established Chosen Tokushu Kagaku Kabushiki Kaisha, capitalized at 1 million yen, and planned to use the plant to manufacture borax.

Borax was an essential material for the manufacture of optical weapons, but manufacturers in Japan had always been forced to rely on imports. During the war, kotoite was discovered in a mine in the upper reaches of the Daedong River, and Hitachi developed the technology to manufacture borax from the ore taken from this mine. Using this technology, the company produced borax at the Incheon Cast Steel Plant, which was part of its group. Later, it built facilities at its plant in Pyongyang, which was located closer to the mining site, with the intention of gearing up mass production. However, only some of the equipment was operating when the war ended.

Plants were either expanded or newly built in many other fields, including electrodes, oil refining, cement, and pulp. Electrodes are needed in large quantities for the manufacture of special steel, light metals, carbide, explosives, and chemical materials, as well as for use in searchlights and power generators. Aluminum plants consume large quantities of positive electrodes in particular. After war broke out between Japan and the United States, demand for electrodes in Korea skyrocketed in the steelmaking, light metals, and electrochemical industries, particularly in early 1944. Most electrodes had previously been bought from Japan, but the military and government issued directives to increase Korean electrode production so that Korea could be self-sufficient in its electrode supply. Before the war ended, a serious shortage of vein graphite, which was used to make negative electrodes, prompted plans to produce artificial graphite as a substitute. A summary of plants expanded or newly built, including electrode plants, is given in table 4-7.

Table 4 7.

Plant Expansion and New Construction in the Fertilizer, Chemical Materials, Artificial Petroleum, Oil Refining, Electrodes, Papermaking/Pulp, Cement, and Fireproof Brick Sectors

Plant name	Summary
Nippon Chisso Heungnam Fertilizer Plant	Steadily expanded after its founding, it manufactured ammonium sulfate, ammonium sulfate phosphate, calcium superphosphate, calcium cyanamide, and other products; it shipped large amounts both inside Korea and to Japan. At the end of the war, it was operating 24 ammonia synthesis towers and employed 7,918 workers (of whom 2,402 were Japanese). Annual production capacities were 190,000 tons of ammonia, 600,000 tons of sulfuric acid, and 500,000 tons of ammonium sulfate. In 1943, it had the largest ammonium sulfate production capacity of any similar plant in the Japanese Empire, accounting for 26 percent of the total.
Nicchitsu Nenryo Kogyo Cheongsu Plant	A Nippon Chisso carbide plant in Cheongsu, below the Supung Dam. Construction began in 1940; operation began in 1943. Equipped with three carbide furnaces and the latest facilities capable of automated operation.
Nicchitsu Gomu Kogyo Namsan Plant	Nippon Chisso founded Nicchitsu Gomu Kogyo under order from the Navy in 1942, and the new company built a synthetic rubber plant next to the carbide plant in Cheongsu. The plant synthesized rubber from acetylene. Commercialization was achieved just before the war ended.
Chosen Jinzo Sekiyu Aoji Plant	In 1940, Chosen Sekitan Kogyo renamed its Hoeam Plant "Aoji Plant." In 1941, the company changed its own name to Chosen Jinzo Sekiyu and pursued coal liquefaction. Overcoming technical challenges, it achieved continuous operations that far surpassed those of the leading German chemical company, IG Farben. In 1943, under a directive from the Navy, it stopped producing liquefaction oil and began producing methanol for use in fuel for naval planes. Its annual methanol production capacity was 16,000 tons, some of which was delivered to the arsenal in Mukden (present-day Shenyang) in southern Manchuria.
Chosen Sekiyu Wonsan Oil Refinery	In 1935, Nippon Sekiyu founded Chosen Sekiyu with a capitalization of 10 million yen. The same year, it constructed an oil refinery that began operating in 1936, with a production capacity larger than that of mid-sized refineries in Japan. Products included aviation fuel, gasoline, aviation lube oil, and heavy oil. Production facilities were later expanded to a capitalization of 50 million yen and a yearly oil production capacity of 400,000 cubic meters at the end of the war.

Plant name	Summary
Nihon Tanso Kogyo Seongjin Plant	In 1940, Nippon Carbon and Nihon Koshuha Jukogyo invested equally to found Nihon Tanso Kogyo with a capitalization of 2.5 million yen. Nippon Carbon dispatched engineers to construct an electrode manufacturing plant, part of which began operating in 1942. The plant was completed in 1943. The natural and artificial graphite electrodes produced there were delivered to Nihon Koshuha Jukogyo Seongjin Plant.
Chosen Tokai Denkyoku Jinnampo Plant	In 1940, Tokai Denkyoku Seizo (a subsidiary of Daido Seiko), in conjunction with Hosen Muentanko Kabushiki Kaisha in Korea, founded Chosen Tokai Denkyoku with a capitalization of 5 million yen. Construction started in August of that year with the support of the Government-General. In July 1943, full operation began with an electrode production capacity of 4,800 tons per year. The electrodes produced there were delivered to Mitsubishi Seiko Pyongyang Works and Chosen Seitetsu Pyongyang Works. Raw materials included vein graphite, earthy graphite, and anthracite from Korea, as well as pitch coke from Japan and northern China. In 1944, a decision was made to expand the facility. Construction began with borrowed equipment including a 2,000-ton press and high-voltage electrical equipment from the parent company Tokai Denkyoku, and kneading machines and other equipment from Chosen Denko Jinnampo Plant. Construction was half-way completed when the war ended.
Showa Denko Pyongyang Plant	In April 1944, under the direction of the Ministry of Munitions, Showa Denko began building a plant with the capacity to produce 20,000 tons of artificial graphite per year. Plans called for the installation of equipment with a 10,000-ton production capacity during the first phase of construction. For raw material, the plant was to use earthy graphite and anthracite sourced near the Pyongyang suburbs, with the finished product shipped to Japan. When the war ended, the building was nearly completed and the project was awaiting the arrival of machinery produced by Hitachi Seisakusho in Japan.
Oji Seishi (Oji Pulp) Sinuiju Plant	Near the end of the war, the Government-General adopted a policy of Korean self-sufficiency in newsprint. Accordingly, paper-making equipment was transferred from Oji Seishi Tomakomai Plant in Japan to Sinuiju Plant in Korea. Still under construction when the war ended, it had an annual paper production capacity of 15,000 tons.

Plant name	Summary
Kanegafuchi Kogyo Sinuiju Rayon Pulp Plant	In the 1930s, Kanebo developed technology to manufacture rayon pulp from reeds. In 1939, Kanegafuchi Kogyo built a plant to produce rayon pulp from reeds in Sinuiju, near the mouth of the Yalu River where large quantities of reeds grew. The facility had an annual production capacity of 6,000 tons of reed pulp used to make paper and rayon.
Hokusen Seishi Kagaku Kogyo Gilju Plant	In the 1930s, Oji Seishi developed technology for manufacturing alcohol from pulp waste liquid. In 1943, under military order, Gilju Plant added a facility to produce 20,000 tons of alcohol per year. At the time the war ended, the plant had a rayon pulp production capacity of 33,000 tons.
Kanegafuchi Kogyo Pyongyang Rayon/Staple fiber Plant	In 1939, Kanebo planned the construction of a rayon/staple fiber plant. By the end of the war, the plant had a daily production capacity of ten tons of sulfuric acid and thirty tons of rayon/staple fiber. In June 1945, by order of the Fifth Naval Fuel Arsenal in Pyongyang, four out of eight carbon disulfide refining units in the plant were converted for the production of pine-root oil.
Onoda Cement Samcheok Plant	In 1938, Onoda Cement planned the construction of a new plant in Samcheok, Gangwon-do, in the eastern part of southern Korea. The first phase of construction was completed in 1942. It had a production capacity of 150,000 tons per year.
Chosen Asano Cement Bongsan Plant	In 1940, Asano Cement transferred two rotary kilns from its Saiki Plant in Kyushu, Japan, to its Bongsan plant in northern Korea. Annual production capacity was increased to 300,000 tons.
Oryokuko Suiryoku Hatsuden Seunghori Clinker Plant and Supung-dong Cement Plant	In 1940, Oryokuko Suiryoku Hatsuden built a facility to manufacture clinker (an intermediate material for cement) on the grounds of Onoda Cement Pyongyang Plant. The facility included the largest rotary kiln in the Japanese Empire, measuring 145 meters long. The annual clinker production capacity was 170,000 tons. The clinker was crushed at a facility on the construction site of the Supung Dam. In 1939–40, the crushing facility began operating two rotary kilns with an annual cement production capacity of 200,000 tons.
Nippon Magnesite Kagaku Kogyo Seongjin Plant	In 1935, Nihon Koshuha Jukogyo established Nippon Magnesite Kagaku Kogyo with a capitalization of 1 million yen. In 1936, the new company built a refractory and magnesia clinker plant. In 1939, capitalization was increased to 4 million yen. When the war ended, the plant had a magnesia clinker production capacity of 30,000 tons per year.

Plant name	Summary
Nippon Taika Zairyo Milyang Plant and Bongung Plant	In 1937, Nippon Chisso financed the founding of Nippon Taika Zairyo (headquartered in Seoul and capitalized at 500,000 yen). In 1938, the new company built a brick plant in Milyang, Gyeong-sangnam-do, in southern Korea. Capitalization was increased in 1942, and the same type of plant was built in Bongung in northern Korea. In 1944, capitalization was increased to 6 million yen and construction was begun to expand the facilities at both plants. When the war ended, construction was still in progress at the plant in Bongung. The plants had a magnesia clinker production capacity of 28,080 tons per year.
Chosen Shinagawa Shirorenga Dancheon Plant	In 1942, Shinagawa Shirorenga (a leading Japanese fireproof brick company established in 1875) founded, under military order, Chosen Shinagawa Shirorenga (capitalized at 4.5 million yen). The new company built a plant in Dancheon, Hamgyeong-nam-do, in northern Korea. Transporting magnesite on an exclusive railway from the Chosen Magnesite Kaihatsu Yongyang mine, the plant began manufacturing various types of magnesia clinker in 1944–45.

Source: Kimura and Abe 2003, chap. 3.

Production Capacity

In contrast to agricultural production, mining and manufacturing production increased in Korea after 1940. Although the increase occurred primarily in northern Korea, it also happened in southern areas such as Seoul, Incheon, and Busan. Major factors in growth were investments from Japan and a massive input of new labor. Near the end of the war, however, further increases became very difficult to achieve as facilities deteriorated and shortages of parts grew more severe.

As shown in table 4-8, by the end of 1944, Korea had become a large production center of basic materials and thus an essential region for the Japanese Empire in its pursuit of total war.

Table 4-8.

Production Capacities for Basic Raw Materials at the End of 1944:
The Japanese Empire as a Whole and Korea

Product	Unit	A. Overall imperial production capacity	B. Korean production capacity	C. Proportion (%)
Ordinary pig iron	1,000 tons	5,751.0	822.0	14.3
Raw iron for steelmaking	1,000 tons	315.3	81.0	25.7
Aluminum	1,000 tons	196.9	32.3	16.5
Magnesium	1,000 tons	11.0	3.9	35.5
Zinc	1,000 tons	82.0	11.0	13.4
Fluorite	1,000 tons	120.2	61.0	50.7
Asbestos	1,000 tons	15.5	5.5	35.5
Mica	1,000 tons	0.5	0.2	34.8
Vein graphite	1,000 tons	57.4	30.6	53.3
Earthy graphite	1,000 tons	136.2	73.0	53.6
Iron ore	1 million tons	11.0	4.1	35.0
Tungsten ore	1,000 tons	7.0	6.0	85.7
Cobalt ore	1,000 tons	0.1	0.1	100.0
Nickel ore	1,000 tons	20.0	20.0	100.0
Ammonium sulfate	1,000 tons	1,403.0	468.0	33.0
Calcium cyanamide	1,000 tons	174.0	24.5	14.1
Carbide	1,000 tons	444.4	110.0	24.8
Methanol	1,000 tons	36.7	11.5	31.1
Acetylene black	1,000 tons	6.0	3.7	61.6
Dilute nitric acid	1,000 tons	86.4	20.0	23.1
Cement	1 million tons	5.2	1.2	23.0
Grinding materials	1,000 tons	14.3	1.7	12.0
Oxygen	1 million cubic meters	4.0	2.7	68.7
Limestone	1 million tons	17.7	3.0	17.0
Industrial salt	1,000 tons	179.3	25.0	13.9

Product	Unit	A. Overall imperial production capacity	B. Korean production capacity	C. Proportion (%)
Common salt	1,000 tons	561.4	320.0	57.0
Coal	1 million tons	56.4	7.1	12.6

Note: In the original materials, column A gave production capacities for "all of Japan," which did not include Manchukuo. Values in columns A and B were as of December 5, 1944, but the values for industrial salt, common salt, and coal in column A combine the actual amounts produced in Japan in 1944 with the production capacities in Korea as of the date above. Values in column C are calculated from the raw numbers in columns A and B (before rounding). Products listed in the original materials for which Korean production capacity represented less than 10 percent of total imperial production capacity (10 products, including caustic soda) have been omitted.
Source: Kimura and Abe 2003, 111. (Original materials are found in *Teikoku gikai setsumei shiryo* [Explanatory Material for the Imperial Diet].)

5. Korean "War Economy"

State Control More Widespread than in Japan
and Military Industrialization throughout the Region

Before the Sino-Japanese War erupted in 1937, the Government-General compiled its budgets without outside interference. This became impossible, however, under the wartime system. Like the central government of Japan, the Government-General had no choice but to bend to the will and directives of the military. This was evidenced by the abnormal expansion of public financing.

The economic system changed fundamentally. The introduction of a system of responsibility for production, mobilization and organization of labor, push to increase production, mandated delivery of rice and other crops, state control of farmland and companies, and introduction of material mobilization plans all resulted in the virtual disappearance of market-oriented economic elements, that is, economic activity freely pursued by individuals. In many cases economic control and state management in Korea were implemented after similar policies were put in place in Japan, but in agriculture and related fields, these practices developed further in Korea than they did in Japan. The "integrated management" of landlord-owned agricultural land and the nationalization of rice-polishing plants were not seen in Japan (as noted in chapter 2, rice husking and polishing were not industrialized in Japan).

Utilizing rich mineral supplies, ample electrical power, and a large labor force, military industrialization proceeded more widely and rapidly in Korea than has been commonly recognized by scholars up to now. The development of resources of all kinds was pushed throughout Korea, to be used directly or indirectly for the production of munitions. In northern Korea, production extended to special steel and light alloys, which form the central core of the modern weapons industry, as well as to the development of rocket fuel and uranium ore. Though these facts are not generally known even today in the twenty-first century, they are essential to understanding just how important Korea was to Japan in its war against the United States.

The American military did not bomb Korea. Therefore, in contrast to what happened in Japan, the plants built in Korea remained intact until the end of the war.

Building Self-Reliant Industry

Before the 1930s, most of the materials, machinery, and equipment needed for industrial development in Korea had to be brought in from Japan and the West. During the war, however, industrial growth within Korea heightened its self-sufficiency. Many researchers of Korean history believe that the Korean economy became even more dependent on the Japanese economy during the war, but in fact, the opposite is true.

The Japanese Empire, in preparation for long-term war, set about building a "war economy" in Korea through the construction of military and non-military industries (textiles, sundry goods, foodstuffs, etc.) that operated independently from the mother country. Near the end of the war, the Japanese government planned to promote the transfer of facilities and skilled workers from Japan to Korea and partially implemented those plans.

On the other hand, as the slogan "Korea and Manchuria as One" (*Sen-Man ichinyo*) implies, the economic connections between Korea and Manchuria were strengthened. Plants operating in Korea used large quantities of fuel (especially coking coal) and raw materials purchased from Manchuria, and sold half-finished and finished goods (chemical products, machinery, etc.) to Manchuria. In addition, half of the power generated by the Supung Dam was sent to Manchuria. At the same time, economic ties with northern China also grew stronger, as exemplified by Korea's importation of alumina shale. Near the end of the war, Chinese alumina shale was the mainstay of Korean aluminum production. Although the building of self-reliant industries in Korea and Manchuria was not perfected, it did make substantial progress until the fall of the Empire.

Kobayashi Uneo

Kobayashi Toemon (1869–1929), the father of Kobayashi Uneo (1894–1979), moved to Korea in 1906 and became a successful businessman. He built his fortune in large part by operating mines.

After graduating from the Department of Political Science at Tokyo Imperial University in 1919, Kobayashi Uneo served in the Ministry of Agriculture and Commerce and the Ministry of Commerce and Industry. While there he studied geology, becoming well known as an excellent mining engineer. After his father's death, he took over the family business. In 1934, he founded Kobayashi Kogyo Kabushiki Kaisha with a capitalization of 3 million yen. He subsequently operated tungsten mines throughout Korea and developed its business. In 1939, he also established a smelting works near Seoul.

While running his enterprises, Kobayashi took a passionate interest in education. In 1938, the Mining Department at Kanritsu Keijo Koto Kogyo Gakko (a government industrial college) was separated and set up as an independent institution called Keijo Kozan Senmon Gakko (a government mining college). Kobayashi donated 3 million yen of his personal fortune to the newly established college and also made large donations to three other schools at the time they were founded: Kaishu Kogyo Gakko (in the western part of northern Korea), Shunsen Nogyo Gakko (in the northern part of southern Korea), and Jonan Chugakko (in Seoul). In Japan, Kobayashi also provided funding to the Showa Academy, a private school founded in 1938 by Goto Ryunosuke, who chaired the Showa Research Association (Prime Minister Konoe Fumimaro's brain trust). The Showa Academy invited the top intellectuals of the day to present lectures and pursued the goal of nurturing human resources who would support the future of Japan.

Kobayashi actively recruited Koreans as employees at Kobayashi

Kogyo without discrimination. He did not pay attention to ideology and even accepted people with strong nationalistic and socialist beliefs (a practice that contributed to violent labor disputes at Korea Tungsten Mining, after the war). He also believed in sharing company profits with employees and was generous when paying them bonuses.

After the war, Kobayashi returned to Japan and was punitively purged from government service, but he continued to be active after sanctions against him were lifted, taking part in the founding of a metal smelting company and the operation of educational organizations.

Kobayashi Kogyo's Korean-based assets were confiscated in the south by the US military and placed under the direct control of the South Korean government. In 1949, they were transferred to a private firm, Korea Tungsten Mining, which became a stock company in 1952 (the company president at the time was An Bong-ik, who was an alumnus of the Mining Department at Kanritsu Keijo Koto Kogyo Gakko and had served as head of the Planning Department at Kobayashi Kogyo). During this time, the company extracted tungsten ore from the Sangdong mine for export, providing southern Korea and later South Korea with an important source of foreign currency.

Keijo Kozan Senmon Gakko (a government mining college) was a foundation for the Faculty of Engineering of Seoul National University (now the Department of Energy Resources Engineering of the College of Engineering at Seoul National University). In 1969, Korea Tungsten Mining named Kobayashi an honorary adviser as an expression of respect for him as the company founder and as a tribute to all of his efforts. This was an exceptional event because South Korean companies rarely conferred postwar honors on Japanese who managed their predecessor companies in Korea under Japanese rule. It was an expression of the high regard in which he was held for his contribution to the company, overcoming generational and ethnic differences.

* * *

In 1968, Korea Tungsten Mining, complying with a demand made by South Korean President Park Chung-hee, participated in the founding of Pohang Iron and Steel (the precursor of POSCO, one of the world's largest steelmakers today) by providing personnel, capital, and technology. The first president of Pohang Iron and Steel, Park Tae-joon, previously served as the president of Korea Tungsten Mining beginning in 1964, and his leadership played an important role in growth of the new company. (Park served as a major-general in the Korean Army, later entered politics, became the Prime Minister of South Korea in 2000, and passed away in 2011.)

In postwar North Korea, Kim Il-sung greatly appreciated the tungsten mined at the Baengnyeon ("100-year") mine and renamed it the Mannyeon ("10,000-year") mine as an expression of pride in its longevity. A North Korean publication notes that the area around the mine has developed into a mining city, but production details are unknown. In 1981, Kim Il-sung stated that tungsten ore was indispensable for the machinery industry and that he used large amounts of foreign currency to import it because of shortages.

CHAPTER
5

Emergence of North and South Korea
The Legacy of the Japanese Empire

On August 8, 1945, the Soviet Union declared war on Japan and immediately invaded northern Korea (as well as Manchuria and southern Sakhalin). On August 15, Japan announced its acceptance of the Potsdam Declaration, putting an end to Japanese rule in Korea. This is usually where discussion on Korea under Japanese rule ends, but this book does not stop there.

After 1945, the Korean Peninsula was divided into two antagonistic states: South Korea (officially the Republic of Korea, established in August 1948) and North Korea (officially the Democratic People's Republic of Korea, established in September 1948). What did these two states inherit from Japanese rule, and what did they reject? Which aspects were characterized by continuity and which by discontinuity? The historical significance of Japanese rule cannot be properly understood without considering these questions, but answering them is a daunting task. The purpose of this chapter is to provide a sketch of the issues involved.

Focusing on the north and south separately, I begin by discussing the Japanese industrial legacy. Then I examine continuity and discontinuity of ruling ideology, economic system, and military polices from the Japanese period to the post-war period. Finally, I summarize the contrasting economic performance of North and South Korea, which I mentioned in the Preface.

1. Industrial Legacy: Large-Scale Military Manufacturing

A Substantial Legacy in North Korea

The Japanese Empire left a remarkable developmental legacy in Korea that ranged from the installation of infrastructure such as electric power, railways, and harbors to mining and manufacturing production facilities and agricultural progress.

As previously described, most of the infrastructure, mineral resources, and manufacturing facilities were located in the north. In 1945, total power generating capacity in northern Korea was about six times greater than that in southern Korea. On a per capita basis, it was eleven times greater (table 5-1). In fact, on that basis, northern Korea had more power generating capacity than Japan. Since per capita GDP in northern Korea was lower than that in Japan, this indicates that in proportion to economic scale (GDP), northern Korea had more power generating capacity than Japan.

Northern Korea also had more miles of railway track per capita and per unit land area than southern Korea (table 5-2). Although it had less than half of the track length per unit land area in Japan, northern Korea had more track length per capita, making its railway network more developed in terms of the total population.

Compared with the north, the south had only a few richer deposits of mineral resources, including wulfenite, kaolin (used in the ceramics industry), and alunite. Deposits of anthracite, tungsten ore, silver, and gold were widely distributed throughout Korea, but they were more plentiful in the north. Most of the important minerals were produced only in the north, including iron, magnesite, barite, mica, and phosphorus, as well as rare metals such as uranium, cerium, zircon, and titanium.

A lack of data makes it impossible to accurately outline the industrial production capacity in the north and south at the time of the war's end. Table 5-3 shows power consumption in each industrial sector in 1944, which helps delineate production output. About 90 percent of total Korean electric power was consumed in northern Korea in that year, of which 80 percent was consumed by chemical plants. Power consumption in the south outpaced that in the north in just three sectors: textiles, machinery and appliances, and foodstuffs. Even if we combine the power consumption of all three of these sectors, however, the total is less than the amount of power consumed by the single sector of metalworking in the north. These figures show that the north far outpaced the south in the heavy and chemical industries. As discussed in detail in the previous chapter, the heavy and chemical industries in northern Korea were completely oriented toward munitions in the late stages of

Table 5-1.

Power Generating Capacities in Northern Korea, Southern Korea, and Japan in 1945

	A. Total capacity (MW)	B. Population (1,000 people)	C. Per capita capacity (KW)
Northern Korea	1,515	9,379	162
Southern Korea	237	15,975	15
Japan	10,385	72,200	144

Note: The figures for total capacity in northern Korea and southern Korea (for completed facilities) do not include in-house power generating capacity, but the figure for Japan does. The population figure for Japan is the total number of residents of Hokkaido, Honshu, Shikoku, and Kyushu. The Hwacheon Power Plant (with output of 90 MW) on the Han River system is located slightly north of the 38th parallel, but because the electricity it generated was transmitted to Seoul and Incheon, it was included in the figures for southern Korea.
Source: Kimura and Abe 2003, 116.

Table 5-2.

Railway Networks in Northern Korea, Southern Korea, and Japan in 1945

	A. Total length (km)	B. Length per capita (km)	C. Land area (1,000 km^2)	D. Length per km^2 (km)
Northern Korea	4,009	0.43	121	0.033
Southern Korea	2,488	0.16	99	0.025
Japan	25,380	0.35	370	0.069

Note: The figure in column A for Japan indicates operated kilometers, while those for northern Korea and southern Korea represent the total of opened and closed lines. The figures in column C for northern Korea and southern Korea reflect areas north and south, respectively, of the Demilitarized Zone (DMZ) from 1953 onward. In column A, the distance from the 38th parallel to Seoul is included in the total length for northern Korea. This means that the total length for northern Korea is overestimated and that for southern Korea is underestimated. For convenience, land area figures in column C represent the DMZ division of land, not the 38th parallel. Only minor inaccuracies result from these calculation methods.
Source: Kimura and Abe 2003, 119.

Table 5-3.

Power Consumption in Northern Korea and Southern Korea
by Industrial Sector, 1944

(million kWh)

	Textiles	Metalworking	Machinery and appliances	Ceramics	Chemicals	Foodstuffs	Mining	Total (including other unspecified sectors)
Northern Korea	5	105	5	35	1,297	10	116	1,608
Southern Korea	30	14	29	2	8	29	35	181
Total	35	119	34	37	1,305	39	151	1,789

Note: Consumption is broken down by power customer contracts in each sector. Unspecified sectors include lumber milling, printing/bookbinding, agriculture, marine products, and miscellaneous industries. Though not specified in the original source material, it is assumed on the basis of the number of customer contracts (totaling 45,000) that the figures do not include household power consumption.
Source: Chosen Ginko Chosabu 1948, III, 174–177.

the war. So, the Japanese Empire left a substantial legacy there in terms of military manufacturing.

Foodstuff Production Capacity that Could Sustain Life

Because there was considerable fluctuation between good and bad harvests from year to year, it is difficult to accurately indicate production capacity in the agricultural sector. As already discussed, rice production in northern Korea increased at a high rate under Japanese rule. Nevertheless, it never produced more than the south. From the late-1930s, annual rice production in the north averaged 30 to 40 percent of that in the south. Since the north had approximately half the population of the south, the south produced more rice even on a per capita basis.

If we look at foodstuffs in general (including rice, wheat and barley varieties, minor grains, legumes, and potatoes), the north produced slightly more than half the total produced in the south, because the north produced relatively more minor grains and potatoes. Viewed in aggregate, then, we find that the north did in fact surpass the south in terms of per capita foodstuff production capacity. Although per capita food production slumped in the north from 1942 to 1944, it still maintained an average annual production of about 260 kilograms per capita, or about 700 grams per capita per day. Assuming that all of the produce was allocated to the people, this was a level that would not result in starvation. In other words, after the fall of the Japanese Empire, northern Korea was left a food production capacity that could sustain the population.

2. Continuity and Discontinuity between the Wartime and Postwar Eras

Continuity in the North and Discontinuity in the South

After the war, Korea was divided at the 38th parallel north into two occupied zones, with the Soviet Union in the north and the United States in the south. Concerning the period of military occupation and subsequent creation of nation states, it is generally argued that, at least from the perspective of personnel, the south pursued a path of continuity while the north opted for discontinuity. It is certainly true that Koreans who cooperated with Japan, the so-called pro-Japan faction, continued to wield political, social, and economic power in South Korea after the war. It is also true that Syngman Rhee, who emerged as a new political leader, had been part of an anti-Japanese independence movement in the United States, as had Kim Gu in China. But they were exceptions.

In contrast, Koreans who had been in power under Japanese rule in the north were thoroughly purged. Landowners who had held the reins of power in rural areas since the Korean dynasty period were banished to the hinterlands under land reform implemented in March 1946. Company managers and other wealthy people in the cities were stripped of power by means of currency reform instituted in December 1947, where new currency was issued to replace the old currency issued by Chosen Ginko. The Soviet military authorities meticulously prepared the reform behind closed doors and implemented it suddenly. An extremely low upper limit was placed on the amount of currency that could be exchanged, so that people whose wealth was denominated in the old currency lost their assets. In addition, the people who became political leaders in postwar North Korea were communists who had previously been practically invisible, having fled to the Soviet Union, China, Manchuria, or were hiding in Japan or Korea during Japanese rule.

Indeed, these facts are important. But in the following discussion, I review how, in other aspects, North Korea actually opted for continuity whereas South Korea chose to disrupt its connection with the colonial past.

Ideology: Totalitarianism and Liberalism
North

Communism (Marxism) and anti-communist nationalism (fascism) appear to be completely opposite ideologies. This is not necessarily true, however, insofar as they share a commitment to totalitarianism or collectivism. At the heart of totalitarianism is the idea that the free, individualized exercise of political and economic activity should be prohibited, and that all authority should be concentrated in the state. Communism and anti-communist nationalism share this tenet.

This can be understood through the simultaneous feelings of antagonism and affinity that prewar Japanese nationalists had for communism. On this point, the following observations by Miyazaki Masayoshi (director of the Nichi-Man Zaisei Keizai Kenkyukai [Research Institute on

Public Finance and Economy in Japan and Manchuria], which worked with the Kwantung Army to plan and implement economic administration in Manchuria) are very suggestive.

> Marxist thought has given great impetus to the world of thought in Japan, with an unprecedented influence on all strata of politics, economics, and culture. It has completely permeated the Japanese intelligentsia, and its revolutionary theory gives the impression of being scientific . . . [so that] some have fanatically believed in it as the most authoritative reform theory. Although the factions on the right denounce Marxism, their national reform theory is influenced or even dominated by Marxism to a large degree, to the point where the extreme right is separated from the extreme left by the mere thickness of a single sheet of paper. (Miyazaki 1938, 124)

Near the end of the war, the Nichi-Man Zaisei Keizai Kenkyukai formulated its own plan to reform the state, which garnered some military support. The plan, which included the collectivization of agriculture, was almost indistinguishable from communism, demonstrating that the more extreme anti-communist nationalism becomes, the more it comes to resemble communism.

After the fall of the Japanese Empire, the political system in the north was transformed without serious disruption. One reason for this was the similarity between anti-communist nationalism and communism. No fundamental change was required in the concept or spirit of rule to achieve the transition. In prewar Korea, the spirit of liberalism was even weaker than it was in Japan. During the war, the market economy and system of free enterprise that had substantially developed to that point were destroyed, paving the way for totalitarianism to dominate politics, society, thought, and the economy. The Soviet Union merely transplanted communism on top of that. Therefore, after a relatively small number of dissenting factions (intellectuals committed to liberalism, religious [especially Christian] adherents, and business entrepreneurs) were purged, there were no major factors left to disturb North Korea's regime. From the perspective of totalitarian ideology, then, there was continuity in the north between the wartime and postwar eras.

South

In the south, the American military dismantled the Japanese Empire's totalitarian state and worked to transplant or encourage the growth of liberalism (and democracy). Subsequently, Syngman Rhee, an anti-communist liberal who had received his higher education in the United States and shared the same basic philosophy, took over the reins of government. This meant a complete transformation of ruling principles, and it was the basic reason that the process of decolonialization was much more disruptive in the south than it was in the north. In the south, various factions competed for power, influenced by liberalism, communism, anti-communist nationalism, traditionalism/reactionism, and religion. Their respective interests often clashed, creating deep societal fractures. Syngman Rhee exercised autocratic authority to suppress anti-government elements, especially communism, but he was unable to prevent conflict and division.

In 1961, Park Chung-hee seized power through a military coup. Aiming to reconstruct a strong state, Park set out to reform the liberal system. While pursuing government-led industrialization and bank nationalization, he also developed a movement to encourage a national spirit, as exemplified by the *Saemaeul Undong* (New Village Movement). Park's policies were quite similar to those pursued by the Japanese Empire during the war and by postwar North Korea. Park was a military man who had received his education at the Manchurian Military Academy and the Imperial Japanese Army Academy. He harbored both strong hatred and grudging respect for Japanese rule. This combination of elements in his personality is largely responsible for the influence that the Imperial Japanese Army had on his thought, action, and ruling methods, beginning with the military coup itself.

However, the influence of the Imperial Japanese Army should not be overemphasized. Park learned a great deal from the Meiji Restoration in Japan and revolutions that occurred in developing countries. He also spent a short time in 1954 as an exchange student in the United States. The things he learned were very different from those learned by his North Korean counterpart Kim Il-sung. In fact, South Korea under Park's administration was led by neither totalitarianism nor a cult of personality. He accepted many value systems, as long as they were anti-communist. Even before the Park regime crumbled in 1979, the South Korean people, influenced by American democracy, made increasingly strong demands for political freedom. This trend came to rule South Korea in subsequent years. This means that the south, having experimented with a systemic transition that contrasted sharply with that of the north, experienced great turmoil after August 1945 but finally achieved the transition decades later.

Controlled Economy and Market Economy
North
Under Soviet military occupation, the north became subject to state control policies that had been pursued by the Japanese Empire during the war. These policies were originally formulated under Soviet influence. Those who played leading roles were members of the so-called "Control Faction" (*Tosei-ha*) of the Imperial Japanese Army and reformist bureaucrats (*kakushin kanryo*) who were affiliated with the faction. As is well known, they studied the political and economic control and planning policies pursued by the Soviet Union (and the Nazis) in the 1930s and applied them to Manchuria and eventually the Japanese Empire. For this reason, the Soviet occupation forces were deeply familiar with the control policies implemented in the north.

In August 1946, the Soviet military authorities nationalized all of the main former Japanese companies in the north. Initially, they allowed small and medium-sized traders and manufacturers to continue to conduct business. This was a temporary, strategic policy designed to soften Korean antipathy to Soviet military rule. To win the support of tenant farmers, the authorities announced that the land reform was the "material base for establishing a progressive democratic society." The word "socialism" was consciously avoided because of its associations with the confiscation of agricultural land by the state. This policy is specifically mentioned in North Korean internal documents from the time (Communist Party of Korea, North Korea Branch, Propadanda Department 1946, 5).

As a result of the reform, tenant farmers were given landownership rights, but they quickly discovered that these were a mere formality. Not only were the sale and rental of farmland prohibited, but severe restrictions were placed on crop selection and the sale of harvested produce. In this respect, the land reform was of a piece with the changes in landownership pursued by the Japanese Empire near the end of the war. As such, it made an important and large step toward achieving the Soviet military's aims of strengthening control over the entire economy and nationalizing all assets.

With the founding of the North Korean state, the Kim Il-sung regime continued these policies and developed them further. After the Korean War, additional progress was made on the collectivization of agriculture and small and medium-sized businesses, with every sector of the economy placed under government control. With this, a system of full national mobilization of human and material resources was completed. Thus, reforms of the economic system that were pursued during World War II by a faction of the Imperial Japanese Army and the reformist bureaucrats were finally realized by the Kim Il-sung regime in the 1950s.

South

The American military government in the south initially banned many governmental controls and gave attention to fully resurrecting the market economy. As part of this effort, companies and plants formerly owned by Japanese nationals were sold off to the private sector as "reverted property," and the sale of cereal grains was liberalized. The sale of reverted property generated serious political problems in terms of

choosing buyers and setting prices, but the American military authorities, aiming at the development of a market economy, did not change
course.

However, liberalization policies were soon revoked (beginning in the
autumn of 1945). Farmers were forced to sell their cereal grains to the
government, which then distributed them among the people. At first
glance, these policies seem to resemble those adopted in the north, but
the basic underlying stance was different. Even though free transactions
were the ideal, when essential goods for human life were involved, the
inadequate supply system had to be put under certain distribution and
consumption controls. The American military's intention was ultimately
based on ensuring urban residents enough grain to eat; it was not to
reconstruct the controlled economy.

The economic policies of Syngman Rhee were not primarily founded
on laissez-faire as commonly defined. They permitted a wider range of
control compared with the policies of the American military authorities,
but they did share with the American approach a foundation on the
market economy. Although the Park regime did actively intervene in
the economy, it never denied a system of private property. The administration used the talents of bureaucrats who received their education in
the United States, and it pursued economic policies that fundamentally
relied on market mechanisms.

Militarization and Demilitarization
North
In terms of economic construction, the essence of Soviet military rule,
which was adopted by Kim Il-sung, was the activation and further development of the military industry left behind by the Japanese Empire.
Soviet occupation forces seized grain and inventories of industrial raw
materials and finished and half-finished products in the north and sent
them to the Soviet Union. They also dismantled plant facilities and took
them away. These actions were only taken in the early years, however,
and their scale was limited (unlike what happened in Manchuria and

East Germany). Later, the Soviets put interned Japanese engineers to work reviving industry in the north.

Kim Il-sung entered Korea with the Soviet military in September 1945 and energetically inspected the factories Japan had left behind. One of the first plants he focused on was Pyongyang Munitions Plant, which he planned to expand, calling it by the code name Plant No. 65. After the North Korean state had been established, the Kim Il-sung regime invested a great deal of effort in expanding armaments. In 1949, it built its first coast guard vessel at Wonsan Dockyard, which was the successor to Chosen Zosen Kogyo Wonsan Dockyard, which had been in operation since before the war. The steel plate used to build the coast guard ship was manufactured by Hwanghae Ironworks (formerly Nippon Seitetsu Gyeomipo Ironworks).

In March 1949, Kim Il-sung visited the Soviet Union and signed a treaty on economic and cultural cooperation. A secret agreement was attached to this treaty, which contained a commitment on the part of the Soviet Union to supply North Korea with large amounts of weapons. The Soviet Union also promised to provide assistance for the construction of TNT gunpowder factories and underground munitions plants.

Meanwhile, Kim Il-sung ordered increased production of minerals, particularly lead and zinc. These minerals were essential not only for domestic weapons production but for export to the Soviet Union. The Soviet Union did not provide weapons, capital goods, and technical guidance free of charge. It demanded compensation. To pay what it owed, the Kim Il-sung regime had to increase its exports of lead and zinc to the Soviet Union. Similarly, it exported large amounts of monazite and columbite. Some argue that the Soviet Union used these uranium-containing ores to manufacture atomic bombs (Shimotomai 2004, 31).

In June 1950, the Korean People's Army crossed the 38th parallel and invaded South Korea (under the pretext of defending the homeland from invasion from the south). This act, which utilized weapons that were manufactured both in North Korea and the Soviet Union, was carried out with the tacit approval of the Soviet Union and China, the two communist states supporting North Korea. Today, much of the literature notes that, after the Korean War, Kim Il-sung initiated the policy of "fortifying the entire nation" and promoted building facilities underground. In fact, however, he began this activity during the Korean war, in an undertaking that can fairly be defined as a partial continuation of the military policy originally adopted by the Japanese Empire.

Kim was also intensely interested in developing nuclear weapons that would enable him to strike South Korea, defend against the United States, and eventually unify the Korean Peninsula under his communist regime. In his view, Imperial Japan's legacy of uranium ore development and heavy/chemical industry made such an enterprise entirely feasible. After the Korean War, Kim signed an agreement with the Soviet Union regarding cooperative nuclear research and dispatched a number of researchers to a nuclear research facility on the outskirts of Moscow (Zhebin 2000). Around 1957, a North Korean physicist who had studied in Japan prior to World War II approached the University of Tokyo with a proposal to engage in the joint research of nuclear power (*Koan Chosa Geppo* 6, no. 5, 1957, 111). This information provides corroboration that in the second half of the 1950s, Kim was already planning nuclear development.

South

American occupation forces adopted the basic policy of demilitarizing the Japanese Empire. As they did in Japan itself, they dismantled military plants in the south and promoted a transition to an economy centered on civilian demand. This approach was symbolized by the order to destroy steelmaking facilities and products used for weapons at Mitsubishi Seiko Incheon Plant. The American forces also destroyed weapons and ammunition at the Incheon Army Arsenal, and ordered that Chosen Kikai Seisakusho begin manufacturing small steamboats instead of weapons. Japanese engineers were quickly repatriated, a factor that slowed industrial recovery in the south. The disorderly sale of old Japanese companies to the private sector exacerbated the problem.

It was not until August 1948, after South Korea had been established as a nation, that weapons factories in the south were redeveloped. In 1949, Chosen Yushi Gunpowder Plant in Incheon was reconstituted as a weapons factory. It took even longer to reorganize the overall armory, a task that was not addressed until 1950.

The withdrawal of US troop and South Korea's delayed military development were two major factors that triggered North Korea's invasion. Subsequently, the construction of a system to resist North Korea's military and non-military aggression became the supreme political issue, determining the life or death of the state. Addressing that issue, however, had to wait for the birth of Park Chung-hee's military regime.

3. North Korea's Long-Term Stagnation and South Korea's Miraculous Prosperity

Contrasting Postwar Paths

After World War II, North Korea inherited a huge industrial legacy from the Japanese Empire, along with totalitarianism and a state-controlled economy. It used these as the bedrock for state operations under the name of socialism or communism. Whether it takes the form of communism or anti-communist nationalism, totalitarianism is characterized by priority given to military build-up and expansionism. These traits were conspicuous in the Soviet Union under Stalin and in Nazi Germany, and they could also be found in the Japanese Empire in the second half of the 1930s and the 1940s.

Influenced by the Soviet Union and the Japanese Empire, the Kim Il-sung regime added uniquely Korean elements (such as Confucian traditionalism) and built a state that prioritized the military. After it failed to expand into South Korea through a military attack, it continued its offensive against the south through terrorist attacks and political maneuvering. Kim Il-sung's successor Kim Jong-il placed even greater emphasis on strengthening the military under the banner of "military-first politics" and pushed forward with nuclear and missile development.

During all these years, the industrial legacy of Japanese rule, particularly the large-scale power generation plants, chemical industrial complexes, and ironworks, continued to be the mainstay of the North Korean economy. But unproductive investment that was excessively tilted toward the military, coupled with the inefficiencies that accompanied the controlled economy, resulted in long-term stagnation. Furthermore, the regime repeatedly issued chaotic orders to all sectors to increase production while indulging in opulent consumption and ostentatious displays of power. As a result, the economy was "planned" in name only, and with the market economy suppressed, the people regressed to self-subsistence as a means of supporting their livelihoods.

The south also inherited the industrial legacy of Japanese rule. Although it had far fewer power plants and heavy/chemical industries than the north, it had considerable resources in the fields of transport, communications, light industry, and agriculture (as well as commerce and marine products, two categories not addressed in this book). If we include human capital in this list, the resources available to the south expanded even more.

The south worked to achieve a transition from the economic system it inherited from Japanese rule and made full use of its legacy through the market economy. Under the able leadership of the Park regime, South Korea attracted large-scale investment from advanced industrialized countries, introduced technologies, and built an economy that made maximum use of profits from foreign trade. This strategy followed a universal model of development that transcends era and the differences between suzerain and colonized states. Thus, South Korea rose from the devastation of the Korean War to achieve miraculous prosperity, following in the footsteps of Japan and Taiwan in East Asia.

The Legacy of the Roman Law Library
at Keijo Imperial University

When the war ended, Keijo Imperial University comprised the Department of Law and Literature, the Department of Medicine, and the Department of Science and Engineering. It was later combined with other institutions to create Seoul National University, which continued to use Keijo Imperial University's resources, both human and physical. In this column, I introduce the Roman Law Library bequeathed to the university by Professor Funada Kyoji.

Funada Kyoji (1898–1970), originally from Utsunomiya in Tochigi Prefecture and a graduate of the Law Faculty of Tokyo Imperial University, became an associate professor at the Department of Law and Literature of Keijo Imperial University in 1926 and a full professor in 1928. His father Funada Hyogo founded the private school system now called Sakushin Gakuin; his older brother Funada Naka was a well-known politician (a member of the House of Representatives both before and after the war, and chairman of that chamber in the 1960s and 1970s); and his younger brother Fujieda Sensuke was also a politician (a member of the House of Representatives after the war, who also served as minister of transport, minister of home affairs, and vice-chairman of the House).

Funada Kyoji studied Roman Law at Keijo Imperial University and published his *Roma ho* (Roman Law) in 1943–44. Comprising five volumes, this magnum opus received this rave review: "[The author's] effort and energy cannot help but inspire wonder . . . nor can it help but have a huge impact on academia in general and therefore the study of law . . . no work of a commensurate enormous scale can be easily found, not just in Japan, but anywhere in the world." (Harada 1946, 33.)

Funada's work referenced a vast number of books in various European languages. These included particularly precious volumes that originally belonged to famous law scholars in Germany and Austria. Funada acquired these books in 1937 and placed them in the library at Keijo Imperial University. Although it is unclear exactly how he acquired them, it is said that some of the early volumes were sent to Japan from Germany in lieu of reparations after World War I. The fact that Japan did receive ships, dyes, and radios from Germany instead of monetary war reparations is confirmed in articles published in the *Asahi Shimbun* newspaper on June 15, 1922 and April 2, 1926. This makes it entirely possible that books were also sent.

Numbering close to 7,500 volumes and still housed in the Seoul National University library, the collection is a premier resource for the academic circles of law around the world.

After the war, Funada himself returned to Japan and, taking the place of his older brother who had been purged from public office, became a member of the House of Representatives in 1946. After his brother was restored to his political post, Funada returned to academia and published a revised edition of *Roma ho* in 1968. As with its predecessor, the revised edition enjoyed high critical acclaim.

Chapter

6

What Did Japan Gain from Its Rule over Korea?

What Does Statistical Data Tell Us?

In this chapter, I take a different approach and consider this question: what did Japan gain or lose as a result of its rule over Korea? This question is the flip side of the main theme of this book, which is how Korea fared under Japanese rule.

Many people have shown interest in and debated this issue for some time, and rather sharp disagreement can be discerned. One side asserts that Japan reaped tremendous benefit from its rule over Korea, while the other claims that ruling Korea entailed great expense and was a burden on Japan. Which is correct?

It is not an easy question to answer. "Japan" is not a monolithic economic entity. When profits or financial burdens were generated, we must ask who benefitted and who paid the cost. Were they investors (capitalists), industrialists, or workers? Different outcomes may accrue to each of these groups. Unless we investigate them in detail, we cannot have a correct understanding of the advantages and disadvantages that Japan experienced through its rule over Korea.

Economic relationships commonly develop between a colonial power and its colony in such areas as trade, investment, and labor movement. This was the case between Japan and Korea. What effect did these relationships have on each social stratum in Japan?

In what follows, I analyze how these various relationships benefited or harmed industrialists, farmers, workers, investors, and the government on the basis of statistical data. Because of data limitations, the analysis is restricted to 1910–1939.

Trade between Japan and Korea

Japanese manufacturers are said to have had a monopoly on Korea as an export market, which enabled them to increase their profits. But just how important was Korea as a product market?

Looking at Japanese manufacturing as a whole, about 80 percent of products manufactured in Japan were aimed at the domestic market from the 1910s through the 1930s (table 6-1-1). That is, the export market accounted for about 20 percent of the total market. Although Korea's share of that export market did increase beginning in the 1910s, it still only accounted for about 3 percent of the total market in 1935. These data belie the assertion that the Korean market was important to Japanese manufacturing. Certainly, one could find examples of individual Japanese industries that were highly dependent on the Korean market. But even for the often-mentioned cotton industry, Korea was not a major market after annexation (table 6-1-2). Although cotton was an important export industry for Japan before World War II, the main markets were China, British India, and Southeast Asia, not Korea.

Farmers and Workers

Agriculture was one sector in which imports from Korea actually cut into the domestic market for Japanese producers. This was particularly true for rice farming, which competed directly with imported rice from Korea.

Around 1915, imports from Korea represented about 3 percent of total rice production in Japan. That percentage subsequently rose quickly, however, exceeding 13 percent by about 1935 (table 6-2). The influx of rice from Korea was one factor that depressed rice prices, and Japanese rice farmers (both landowners and tenant farmers) sustained a heavy blow as a result. For that very reason, they strongly opposed large-volume (and unlimited) rice imports and attempted to use their political clout to reduce imports. Those efforts culminated in the discontinuation of the Sanmai Zoshoku Keikaku (Rice Production Development Program), Japan's campaign to increase Korean rice production (discussed in chapter 2).

Other things being equal, a fall in commodity prices is a blessing to consumers. Before the war, trends in the price of rice were incomparably more important to ordinary workers than they are today because the proportion of spending on food to total household consumption (Engel's coefficient) was relatively high, and rice was an indispensable staple. If, however, lower rice prices are accompanied by lower wages in

Table 6-1.

Japanese Domestic Manufacturing: Production and Exports

1. Overall

(1 million yen)

	A. Amount produced	B. Exports	C. B/A (%)	D. Exports to Korea	E. D/A (%)
1912	2,496	478	19.2	29	1.2
1925	10,100	2,234	22.1	167	1.7
1935	14,968	2,697	18.0	429	2.9

2. Cotton Textile Industry

	A. Amount produced	B. Exports	C. B/A (%)	D. Exports to Korea	E. D/A (%)
1912	345	96	27.8	12	3.5
1925	1,553	632	40.7	55	3.5
1935	1,617	600	37.1	69	4.3

Sources: Yukizawa and Maeda 1978, 116, 118, 120, 141, 151, 161; and Shinohara 1981, 143, 189, 195.

Table 6-2.

Rice: Japanese Domestic Production and Imports from Korea

(1,000 tons)

	A. Amount produced	B. Imports from Korea	C. B/A (%)
1915	8,006	248	3.1
1925	8,692	780	9.0
1935	9,396	1,273	13.5

Note: Years shown are the central years of five-year averages.
Sources: The Government-General of Korea 1942b, 80; and Agriculture Policy Research Association 1977, 194–195.

a correlated relationship, workers do not reap the benefits of lower rice prices—industrialists (employers) do. The correlation between rice prices and wages was frequently pointed out in debates concerning Japan's industrialization from the 1920s to the 1930s, which some argued, was promoted in part by rice imported from Korea and Taiwan.

The assertion that imported rice promoted industrialization did not, however, pass a rigorous statistical test. According to a test I conducted, no significant correlation existed between the price of rice and wage levels during the period under consideration (Kimura 1995). Ultimately, the beneficiaries of rice imported from Korea to Japan were workers not industrialists.

Did Investment Lead to Huge Profits in Japan?

Japanese investors are said to have reaped great rewards from their investments in Korea. Investment in land is a typical example. In the early years after annexation, those who bought land in regions with fertile rice paddies and operated farms that charged tenant farmers high rents enjoyed rates of return of 10 percent to 20 percent. The average rate of return gradually declined, but it was still nearly 10 percent into the 1930s, or about twice what could be earned on similar investments in Japan.

From the 1910s to the 1930s, Japanese investment in Korea increased greatly, accompanied by an increase in the amount of interest and profit sent to Japan. But if we ask whether or not this added substantially to Japan's national income, the profits paid to overseas investors in total (mostly to Japan) represented less than 0.5 percent of Japan's total national income in the 1930s, and they amounted to less than 1.5 percent of Japan's property income (profit/interest income) in the non-agricultural sector (table 6-3). This was simply because Japanese investment in Korea was not that large when compared with the size of Japan's overall economy.

Table 6-3.

Profits Paid on Overseas Investment in Korea and
Japanese National Income

(1 million yen)

	1930	1935	1939
A. Profits paid on overseas investment	54.1	74.7	105.3
B. Japanese national income	11,740	14,440	25,354
C. A/B (%)	0.46	0.52	0.42
D. Property income (non-agricultural)	4,210	5,017	9,129
E. A/D (%)	1.29	1.49	1.16

Note: National income is the net national product at factor cost. Property income is the gross income of all sectors other than agriculture, minus wage income.
Sources: Ohkawa, Takamatusu, and Yamamoto 1987, 201; Ohkawa and Shinohara 1979, 380; and Yamamoto 1992, 273–275.

Koreans Working in Japan and Japanese Relocating to Korea

After World War I, an increasing number of Koreans entered Japan either as temporary workers or immigrants. This trend accelerated in the 1930s. In 1939, there were about 1 million Koreans living in Japan. This seems large, but it was only 1.5 percent of Japan's total population of 70 million and was not on a scale that affected the Japanese labor market.

Many Koreans lived in and around Osaka, where they engaged in manual labor for low wages. In 1930, about 30 percent of the workers who built roads and railroads in Osaka were Korean. This was enough to lower overall wages paid to construction workers. But even in Osaka in that year, Koreans only accounted for 2 percent of the total workforce and did not have an effect on the overall labor market.

What about the movement of labor from Japan to Korea? During the Meiji period, especially from the 1880s, the government viewed population surplus as a serious social problem because, despite the limited amount of cultivated land in Japan, the population was growing at a rate of hundreds of thousands per year.

After annexation, the government encouraged Japanese farmers to move to Korea, but that policy did not continue long because surveys revealed that Korea did not have large areas of undeveloped land, but rather had a population density similar to that in Japan.

From the time before annexation, various Japanese people lived in Korea, including so-called "fortune seekers" who were hoping to get rich quick. After annexation, the number of Japanese government officials and company employees living in Korea increased. As citizens of the colonizing country, they formed the upper class and enjoyed economic advantages (Kimura forthcoming). Their average incomes were much higher than those of ordinary people in Japan. Thus, one can say that Japanese who moved to Korea were generally the beneficiaries of Japanese rule there. However, there were not many of them. In 1939, a total of 650,000 Japanese lived in Korea, making up less than 1 percent of the total Japanese population.

Was Rule of Korea a Burden on the Japanese Government?

As already discussed, the Japanese government provided the Government-General of Korea with a subsidy from the general account. This covered one category of expenses for ruling Korea. Other expenses (paid directly out of the general account) included pensions for bureaucrats working for the Government-General and military expenses.

Table 6-4.

Financial Burden on the Japanese Government Associated with Ruling Korea

(1 million yen)

	1910–14	1915–19	1920–24	1925–29	1930–34	1935–39
A. Amount of burden	20.7	15.2	33.1	34.9	28.4	11.4
B. Total expenditure from general account	594.0	819.7	1,485.1	1,684.1	1,880.5	2,995.9
C. A/B (%)	3.5	1.9	2.2	2.1	1.5	0.4

Note: See the main text for a breakdown of the amount of burden. Figures for both A and B are annual averages.
Sources: Yamamoto 1992, 268–275; and Bank of Japan 1966, 130–132.

Starting in the 1930s, the Government-General itself began to cover some of the costs associated with government employee pensions and the military. With these amounts subtracted, table 6-4, row A shows the amounts of expenses covered by the Japanese government. As a percentage of total expenditures for the general account, the amount peaked in the first half of the 1910s at 3.5 percent, falling to 2 percent in the 1920s and 0.4 percent by the second half of the 1930s. These figures indicate that the financial burden imposed on the Japanese government by ruling Korea was insignificant in later years.

The burden was passed on to the Japanese people in the form of taxes, but the amount assessed was tiny compared with national income (not shown in the table).

Motivation for Colonization

During Japanese rule, Korea's total population was approximately 30 percent that of Japan. Looking just at that number, one might think Korea was extremely important to Japan for economic reasons. But this was not the case in the years leading up to 1939, as examined in this chapter. With the exception of rice exports, the Korean economy did not have much of an impact on the Japanese economy.

Lenin's theory of imperialism once had a strong influence on Japanese academics. Basing his ideas on Marx's theory of economic determinism and borrowing from Hobson's theory of imperialism, Lenin asserted that highly developed capitalist countries establish overseas colonies with the aim of obtaining locations where they can invest their excess capital. This theory, however, did not apply to the relationship between Japan and Korea, because Japan was not a developed capitalist country and had not yet accumulated excess capital. On the contrary, it usually suffered from a lack of capital. Economic determinism cannot explain Japan's possession of Korea. Indeed, the motivation was political. Taking into account the international situation in East Asia since the Meiji Restoration, it is clear that Japan colonized Korea with the basic intention of ensuring its own security.

Tragic Consequences

Overall, we can say that Japan ruled Korea quite deftly at relatively little cost. I say "deftly" because it succeeded in maintaining public safety and promoted economic growth (which can also be called modernization).

However, in the 1940s, war against the United States changed conditions dramatically. Japan entered a hopeless state of total war that drew Korea into its vortex. Many of the historical problems that persist today between Japan and South Korea, including the issues of so-called comfort women serving Japanese troops and wartime laborers, date from this time.

Ultimately, Japan's defeat in World War II brought an end to Japanese sovereignty in Korea. Japanese nationals living in Korea at the time, including soldiers and others connected with the military, government officials, and private citizens, lost their status and possessions. In northern Korea, many of them even lost their lives. In the name of *hikiage* (withdrawal), they were expelled and forced to move back to Japan empty-handed. Thus, they suddenly fell from being the greatest beneficiaries of Japan's colonization of Korea to being the greatest losers.

The Anti-Colonial Modernization Argument in South Korea:
From the Writings of Professor Han Yeong-u

In recent years, a group of intellectuals in South Korea calling them-selves the "New Right" have actively promoted the idea that Korea mod-ernized under Japanese rule. People with strong leftist and nationalist tendencies have reacted vehemently against this idea. Han Yeong-u (Professor Emeritus of Seoul National University), one of leading mod-ern historians in South Korea, has distanced himself from the critics of the New Right while directly repudiating the New Right's assertions. In the Foreword of his latest book, Professor Han summarizes his basic thought as follows:

> Some on the New Right assert that the period of imperial Japan's oc-cupation of Korea was an era of modernization that made the post-war industrialization and modernization of South Korea possible. This theory is completely mistaken. Were it true, it would be impos-sible to explain why the economy of the north (North Korea), which had many industrial facilities under Japanese occupation, fell behind the economy of South Korea, which did not. (Han 2016, 8.)

Does Professor Han believe that the development or stagnation of an economy is determined solely by what it inherits from previous genera-tions? The quoted passage can be interpreted this way. But certainly, that cannot be. In chapter 3 of the same book (p. 202), Professor Han himself discusses the stagnation of the North Korean economy after the war, noting that the socialist economic structure suppressed the incentive to increase production among residents.

Professor Han is, however, completely against the theory of colonial modernization (p. 300):

The very phrase "colonial modernization" is a contradiction. At the heart of modernization is the "modern nation state." How can a colony that has lost its status as a modern nation state undergo modernization? Like the phrase "ugly beautiful woman," it is an oxymoron.

Consider Taiwan, which became a Japanese colony. What happened under Japanese rule? Physical and systemic infrastructure was developed; institutions associated with medical care, hygiene, and education were established; and industrialization progressed. Today, most Taiwanese identify these changes as modernization. After the war, Taiwan came under the control of the Kuomintang of China led by Chiang Kai-shek and his son Chiang Ching-kuo, who came from the mainland. To the Taiwanese (the original inhabitants), the period of Kuomintang rule was a second era of colonization by a foreign power. Despite this, the Taiwanese economy achieved rapid development. Aside from very peculiar thinkers, everyone recognizes that modernization proceeded even further in postwar Taiwan.

The question of whether or not modernization occurs in a colonized country is an empirical one that cannot be decided ideologically. Like the South Korean history textbooks discussed in Column 2 at the end of chapter 3, Professor Han cites incorrect data concerning rice consumption (p. 127). In this regard, too, his work lacks empirical validity.

Chronology of Korea, 1866–2011
(Dates up to 1887 according to lunar calendar)

Year	Event	Administrator (The Governor-General)
1866	An American ship invades Pyongyang; French warships invade Ganghwa Island (7th and 8th months).	Joseon / Chosen
1871	American warships invade Ganghwa Island (4th and 5th months).	
1875	A Japanese warship exchanges fire with a Korean gun battery on Ganghwa Island (8th month).	
1876	Japan-Korea treaty of amity is signed (2nd month).	
1880	Wonsan Harbor is opened (3rd month).	
1882	Treaties of amity and commerce are signed between Korea and the United States, Great Britain, and Germany (4th and 5th months); Sino-Korean regulations for maritime and overland trade are signed (8th month); Incheon Harbor is opened (11th month).	
1884	Treaty of amity and commerce between Korea and Russia is signed (5th month, intercalary).	
1885	British Eastern Fleet occupies Geomun Island (3rd month to 1st month of 1887).	
1894	Sino-Japanese War begins (July).	
1895	Treaty of Shimonoseki is signed between Japan and China (April).	
1897	Korea changes its name from Joseon to Korean Empire; King Gojong ascends the imperial throne (October).	Korean Empire
1900	Gyeongin Railway begins operation (November).	
1902	Dai-Ichi Ginko's branch office in Korea begins issuing banknotes (May).	
1904	Russo-Japanese War begins (February); First Japan-Korea Convention is signed (August); Megata Tanetaro (Director-General of the Tax Bureau of the Ministry of Finance) becomes a financial adviser to the Korean government (October); Durham Stevens, an American, becomes a diplomatic adviser to the Korean government (December).	
1905	Gyeongbu Railway begins operation; the Currency Ordinance, officially approving the circulation of Japanese currency, is promulgated; Dai-Ichi Ginko is commissioned to engage in a currency readjustment project (January); the Korean government issues bonds in Tokyo worth 2 million yen (June); Second Anglo-Japanese Alliance is signed, recognizing Japan's special interests in Korea (August); Treaty of Portsmouth is signed between Japan and Russia (September); Second Japan-Korea	

Year	Event	Administrator (The Governor-General)
	Convention is signed (November); regulations concerning the Residency-General of Korea and the Resident Offices are promulgated (December).	
1906	Office of the Residency-General of Korea opens (February); Ito Hirobumi arrives in Seoul as the first Resident-General (March); regulations concerning the Railway Administration Bureau of the Residency-General of Korea are implemented (the Japanese government purchases the Gyeongin and Gyeongbu railways) (July).	
1907	The Hague Secret Emissary Affair (in which Emperor Gojong sent envoys to the Hague Peace Conference in the Netherlands to present objections to the unfairness of the Second Japan-Korea Convention, but the envoys were prevented from participating in the conference) occurs (June); Emperor Gojong abdicates; Third Japan-Korea Convention is signed (July); the Korean military is disbanded; the enthronement ceremony of the new emperor (Sunjong) is held (August); disbanded soldiers stage anti-Japanese rebellions throughout the country (from August); the judicial system is reformed (with the promulgation of laws related to the courts); regulations concerning finance, school affairs, agriculture, commerce, and industry are promulgated (December).	Korean Empire
1908	Diplomatic adviser Stevens is assassinated by Koreans because of his support of Japan's presence and protective role in Korea (March); Toyo Takushoku Kabushiki Kaisha is established (August).	
1909	Resident-General Ito steps down and is succeeded by Deputy Resident-General Sone Arasuke (June); Former Resident-General Ito is assassinated by a Korean in Harbin (October); Kankoku Ginko is established as the central bank of Korea (October).	
1910	The Korean government promulgates the Cadastral Survey Act (March); Resident-General Sone steps down and is succeeded by Terauchi Masatake (May); the Japan-Korea Annexation Treaty is signed; the Ordinance Concerning the Establishment of the Government-General of Korea, decrees of amnesty, and regulations concerning reduction of or exemption from land and other taxes are promulgated; an Imperial bounty of 30 million yen is granted (August); regulations concerning the Bureau of Provisional Cadastral Survey are promulgated (September); Terauchi is appointed the governor-general (October); the Company Ordinance is promulgated (December).	Japanese Rule (Terauchi Masatake)
1911	The Act Concerning Korea Industrial Bonds and the Korean Bank (Chosen Ginko) Act are promulgated (March); the Korea Education Ordinance is promulgated (August); construction is completed on the Yalu River Bridge (November).	
1912	The Korea Civil Affairs Ordinance and other ordinances pertaining	

Year	Event	Administrator (The Governor-General)	
	to civil and criminal affairs are promulgated; the Central Laboratory Ordinance, the Korea Tariff Ordinance, and other ordinances are promulgated (March); export taxes on all goods except for eight products (including wheat and soybeans) are abolished (April); the Cadastral Survey Ordinance and the Guns and Gunpowder Control Ordinance are promulgated (August); the Bank Ordinance is promulgated (October).		
1913	Taxes on the importation and transportation of rice and unhusked rice produced in Korea are abolished (Act No. 17) (July); the Ordinance Concerning the Establishment of Cities (*fu*) and the Gakko Kumiai Ordinance (concerning education) are promulgated (October).	Japanese Rule (Terauchi Masatake)	
1914	The Tobacco Tax Ordinance and the Land Tax Ordinance are promulgated; opening ceremony is held for the full length of the Honam Line (March); the Agricultural and Industrial Bank Ordinance and Regional Financial Cooperatives (Chiho Kinyu Kumiai) Ordinance are promulgated (May); opening ceremony is held for the full length of the Gyeongwon Line (September).		
1915	Rice inspection regulations are promulgated (February); technical school regulations are promulgated (March); the Ordinance for the Prevention of Contagious Disease is promulgated (June); the Museum of the Government-General of Korea opens; the Korea Mining Ordinance is promulgated (December).		
1916	Various regulations restricting hostelries and the services of female entertainers and barmaids, as well as the businesses where such services are provided, are promulgated (March); the Ordinance for Implementing Regulations on Corporate Income Tax in Korea is promulgated (July); Governor-General Terauchi steps down and is succeeded by Army General Hasegawa Yoshimichi (October).		
1917	The Ordinance for Entrusting Korean Railway Operations to the South Manchuria Railway Company is promulgated (July); Chosen Heiki Seizosho is established; soybean inspection regulations are promulgated (September); the Ordinance Concerning the Establishment of Villages (*myeon*) is implemented; completion ceremony is held for the Han River Bridge (October); opening ceremony is held for the Hamgyeong Line between Cheongjin and Hoeryeong (November).	Japanese Rule (Hasegawa Yoshimichi)	
1918	The Ordinance Concerning the Prevention of Tuberculosis is promulgated (January); the Ordinance Concerning Revision to the Korea Customs Tariff Act is promulgated; taxes on the import and transport of coal are abolished; exemptions are created on taxes applied to the import and transport of equipment and materials needed by ironworks with a designated production capacity (March); the Suwon Technical School of Agriculture and Forestry is constructed (April); the Korea		

Year	Event	Administrator (The Governor-General)
	Forest Land Survey Ordinance is promulgated (May); Chosen Shoku-san Ginko (Korea Industrial Bank) is established through the merging of regional agricultural and industrial banks; completion ceremony is held for the dock at Incheon Port (October); cadastral survey operations are completed; the Bureau of Provisional Cadastral Survey is abolished (November).	Japanese Rule (Hasegawa Yoshimichi)
1919	Yi Taewang (Gojong) dies (January); the Banzai Sojo Incident (March); a severe drought affects the whole of Korea (July–August); Governor-General Hasegawa steps down and is succeeded by Admiral Saito Makoto; regulations concerning the Government-General of Korea are revised drastically; gendarme-oriented police system is abolished (August); the Government-General of Korea creates the Provisional Drought Relief Commission and implements various anti-drought policies (from September).	
1920	The Company Ordinance is abolished (April); the period of tariff deferment ends (August); a provisional household survey is conducted instead of a national census (October); the educational system is reformed, and student attendance at primary schools is extended to six years (November); the Sanmai Zoshoku Keikaku (Rice Production Development Program) is established; use of old Korean currency is prohibited (December).	
1921	The Tobacco Monopoly Ordinance is enacted; the Monopoly Bureau is established; privately held tobacco factories are acquired (April); the Fishery Experimental Station is established in Busan (May); the Industrial Survey Commission is established (June).	Japanese Rule (Saito Makoto)
1922	The Korea Education Ordinance is revised (February); jurisdiction over the Pyongyang coal field and the Pyongyang Mining Office is transferred from the Government-General of Korea to the Navy Ministry (April); approximately 9,000 White Russian refugees arrive in Wonsan from Vladivostok; the Korean headquarters of the Japanese Red Cross Society is given responsibility for providing aid to the refugees (from October).	
1923	The Korea Vaccination Ordinance is promulgated; the Ordinance for the Prevention of Lung Fluke Disease is promulgated (April); groundbreaking ceremonies are held for the construction of Seongjin and Cheongjin ports (May); jurisdiction over the Army wireless telegraph station in Seoul is transferred to the Communications Bureau (June); approval is given to establish Chosen Tetsudo Kabushiki Kaisha through the merging of private railway companies (September); completion ceremony is held for the Daedong Bridge (November).	
1924	The Government-General of Korea's Fuels and Refining Laboratory	

Year	Event	Administrator (The Governor-General)
	opens (May); a severe drought ravages the rice-producing areas of southern Korea (spring); massive flooding devastates the western part of northern Korea (July); for the first time, a Korean national is appointed to a main government bureau directorship (Educational Bureau); in accordance with policies for streamlining administrative and financial procedures, the number of regular employees is reduced (December).	
1925	The entrustment of railway operations to the South Manchuria Railway Company is revoked (March); the Railway Bureau is newly established; a plan is initiated to increase cocoon production by 1 million *koku* (April); the Security Maintenance Law is implemented in Korea (May); massive flooding devastates the whole of Korea (July–August); a simplified census is implemented (October); telephone service is opened between Korea and Manchuria (November); police and military personnel are dispatched from Korea to ensure the safety of Japanese residing in China (December).	Japanese Rule (Saito Makoto)
1926	Chosen Suiryoku Hatsuden Kabushiki Kaisha is established (January); the Weights and Measures Ordinance, which exclusively employs the metric system, is promulgated (February); the Department of Law and Literature and the Medical Department are established at Keijo Imperial University; an ordinance for implementing parts of the Steel Industry Encouragement Act in Korea is promulgated (April); the Tax Commission is established; relevant regulations are revised to organize national forests and fields and improve both public and private forests and fields (June); a nationwide conference on mountains and forests is convened (October).	
1927	The Ordinance on the Hereditary Property of the Korean Aristocracy is promulgated (February); the Korean Agricultural Association is established; the Ordinance Concerning Korean Capital Interest Tax and Business Tax is promulgated (March); Chosen Chisso Hiryo Kabushiki Kaisha is established; an ordinance on a payment moratorium is promulgated because the financial panic that had struck Japan was affecting Korea; the Land Improvement Department is newly established within the Industrial Bureau (May); the Fertilizer Control Ordinance is promulgated; completion ceremony is held for the International Iron Bridge over the Tumen River (September); the Governor-General Saito steps down and is replaced by Army General Yamanashi Hanzo (December).	
1928	The Provisional Sharecropping Survey Commission holds its first meeting (February); buses run by Keijo-fu (Seoul) begin operating (April); the Government-General of Korea's clinic becomes a hospital attached to Keijo Imperial University (June); the Korea Financial System Research Commission meets (August); the full length of the Hamgyeong	Japanese Rule (Yamanashi Hanzo)

Year	Event	Administrator (The Governor-General)
	Line opens; flooding in Hamgyeong-do results in 1,400 casualties (September); the Coal Field Research Commission holds its first meeting (December).	Japanese Rule (Yamanashi Hanzo)
1929	Notification is issued regarding plans to establish one school in each village (January); opening ceremony is held for the airport in Seoul (April); the Korea Postal Life Insurance Special Account Act is promulgated (May); governmental schools are opened to educate teachers in Daegu and Pyongyang; regulations governing provincial medical training schools are promulgated; regulations governing primary schools are reformed with requirements for vocational training courses (June); Chosen Chochiku Ginko (Korea Savings Bank) is established (July); Governor-General Yamanashi steps down and is replaced by Saito Makoto (August); the Bujeon River Power Plant begins power transmission (November); violence erupts between Japanese and Korean students in Gwangju, resulting in the boycotting of classes throughout Korea (November–December).	
1930	The prohibition of gold exports is rescinded (January); massive flooding throughout Korea results in 2,600 casualties (July); a national census is conducted (October); Chosen Beikoku Soko Kabushiki Kaisha is established (November); extensive reforms are undertaken aimed at local autonomy (December).	Japanese Rule (Saito Makoto)
1931	A completion ceremony is held for renovation work at Unggi Port (May); Governor-General Saito steps down and is replaced by Army General Ugaki Kazushige (June); the Wanpaoshan Incident occurs as violence erupts between Korean farmer immigrants and Chinese residents in the outskirts of Changchun in Manchuria, sparking Korean attacks on Chinese throughout Korea and especially in Pyongyang (July); the Manchurian Incident occurs (September); the prohibition of gold exports is reinstated (December).	
1932	Manchukuo is founded (March); the Northern Korea Development Operations Plan is formulated (April); regulations concerning grain grading stations are promulgated (September); guidelines for the establishment of freehold farmlands are published (October); the Ordinance Concerning Debt Workouts for Financial Cooperative Members is promulgated and implemented; completion ceremony is held for the Tongyeong Canal and Undersea Tunnel (November); the Ordinance on Farm Tenancy Arbitration in Korea is promulgated (December).	Japanese Rule (Ugaki Kazushige)
1933	A ceremony is held to commemorate the opening of telephone service between Japan and Korea; the Provisional Korea Rice Survey Commission holds its first meeting (January); plans to increase raw cotton production are announced (February); plans to promote the development of farming, mountain, and fishing villages are announced; Japan	

Year	Event	Administrator (The Governor-General)	
	withdraws from the League of Nations (March); rail travel between Busan and Sinuiju is sped up (shortened by four hours) (April); the first general elections for provincial legislators are held (May); a five-year plan is adopted for the expansion of salt fields at Kwangryang Bay, and a groundbreaking ceremony is held (June); severe flood damage occurs throughout Korea (June–September); groundbreaking ceremony is held for port construction at Najin; trains begin running directly between Cheongjin and Hsinking (Manchuria) (October); completion ceremony is held for the Geum River Bridge (November).		
1934	Notification is issued concerning the establishment of two-year primary schools (January); the Domestic Sheep Promotion Plan is announced (March); land improvement operations based on the Sanmai Zoshoku Keikaku are discontinued (May); the Korea Farmland Ordinance is implemented (October); trains begin running directly between Busan and Hsinking (November).	Japanese Rule (Ugaki Kazushige)	
1935	A special meeting of provincial governors is held for the purpose of expanding the Farm Household Revival Project (January); the Korea Drug Control Ordinance is promulgated (April); Chosen Tochi Kairyo Kabushiki Kaisha is dissolved (July); a national census is conducted; interdivisional military maneuvers are held in Korea (October); the Jangjin River Hydroelectric Power Plant begins power transmission (November).		
1936	The opening ceremony is held for Keijo Association of Chemistry for National Defense (April); the Senman Takushoku Kaisha Ordinance is implemented (June); Governor-General Ugaki steps down and is replaced by Army General Minami Jiro (August); the Governor-General Minami meets with Kwantung Army Commander-in-Chief Ueda Kenkichi and discusses such matters as practical methods for promoting the "Korea and Manchuria as One" movement (October); the Governor-General Minami meets with Matsuoka Yosuke, President of the South Manchuria Railway Company, and discusses such matters as immigration policy (November); the Ordinance for the Probation of Political Offenders (*Shiso-han*) in Korea is promulgated (December).	Japanese Rule (Minami Jiro)	
1937	The Government-General of Korea and Manchukuo sign a memorandum for the creation of the Korea-Manchuria Yalu River Joint Technology Commission (January); the Law Concerning the Control of Important Industries is implemented (March); the Steel Survey Ordinance is enacted (May); the Chosen Ringyo Kaihatsu Kabushiki Kaisha Ordinance is promulgated (June); the North China Incident (Marco Polo Bridge Incident) occurs, and the Government-General of Korea holds various emergency meetings (July); the Korea Special Taxation Ordinance concerning the North China Incident is promulgated (August); the Ordinance on Korean Gold Production is promulgated (Septem-		

Year	Event	Administrator (The Governor-General)	
	ber); special meetings of provincial governors are held to thoroughly strengthen the National Spiritual Mobilization Movement (December).		
1938	The Provisional Fertilizer Distribution Control Ordinance is implemented (January); the Ordinance Concerning Army Special Volunteers is promulgated (February); the Korea Education Ordinance is revised (March); the National General Mobilization Act is implemented (May); the Ordinance Concerning Increased Production of Important Minerals in Korea is implemented (June); opening ceremony is held for the Kokumin Seishin Sodoin Chosen Renmei (Korean Federation of National Spiritual Mobilization) (July); the Price Committee is established (August); gasoline rationing is implemented (September); maximum price standards are set for coal, briquette, and charcoal (October); plans are made by the Seoul and Incheon municipal governments to create an industrial zone for munitions industries (December).		
1939	The Air Defense Section is newly established within the Police Bureau for the purpose of strengthening air defense (February); the Chosen Magnesite Kaihatsu Kabushiki Kaisha Ordinance is promulgated (April); southern Korea suffers a severe drought (starting in spring); a national registry system is implemented; the National Vocational Ability Declaration Ordinance is implemented; an ordinance to require factories to develop skilled workers is promulgated (June); Seoul and Beijing are connected by telephone landline for the first time (July); the Wage Control Ordinance is implemented (August); a provisional plan is adopted to increase Korean rice production by 3 million *koku*; a maximum rice price is set (September); the Price Control Ordinance, the Rent Control Ordinance, and the National Requisition Ordinance are implemented (October); Chosen Beikoku Shijo Kabushiki Kaisha is established (November); the Farm Rent Control Ordinance is implemented; Mosan Tekko Kaihatsu Kabushiki Kaisha is established (December).	Japanese Rule (Minami Jiro)	
1940	Outline of a plan to increase Korean rice production by 6.8 million *koku* is announced; the Economic Police Section is newly established within the Police Bureau (January); the Marine Transport Control Ordinance is implemented (February); various tax ordinances are reformed, including the Korea Income Tax Ordinance (April); the Heocheon River Hydroelectric Power Plant begins power transmission (May); a plan is adopted to greatly increase the production of barley, soybeans, and other dry-field crops (August); a national census is conducted; guidelines are published for the Kokumin Soryoku Chosen Renmei (Korean Federation for National Total Mobilization) (October); the Ordinance Concerning the Survey of Land Rent Prices is promulgated; guidelines are published for the Rural and Mountain Village Production and Patriotism Campaign (December).		

Year	Event	Administrator (The Governor-General)	
1941	Regulations concerning the subsidizing of aluminum manufacturing are implemented (January); the Preventive Detention Ordinance for Political Offenders in Korea is promulgated; the Provisional Farmland Price Control Ordinance and the Farmland Management Ordinance are implemented (February); implementation guidelines for the Youth Production and Patriotism Campaign are published (March); an oath ceremony is held for implementing production expansion plans for all 70,000 villages in Korea; the Pyeongwon Railway Line begins operation; guidelines for agricultural labor adjustment are published (April); the Korea Housing Corporation Ordinance is promulgated (June); implementation guidelines for the Campaign to Increase Production of Self-supplied Fertilizer are published (July); statistical survey of labor skills is initiated; the Supung Power Station begins power transmission to Manchukuo (August); a second plan to turn tenant farmers into landowners and a plan to increase indirect taxation are published (November); Chosen Sanshi Tosei Kabushiki Kaisha (Korea Raw Silk Control Company) is established (December).	Japanese Rule (Minami Jiro)	
1942	Construction work is begun to expand the water supply for use in the Gyeongin (Seoul and Incheon) Industrial Zone (March); the Amendment Ordinance for Increasing Direct Taxes is implemented; regulations to control planting on Korean agricultural land are implemented; Keiki-do Ryokoku Kabushiki Kaisha is established (April); construction of multiple railway lines between Seoul and Pyongyang is completed; decision made to implement the military draft in Korea; furnace ignition ceremony is held at Nippon Seitetsu's Cheongjin Ironworks; Governor-General Minami steps down and is replaced by Army General Koiso Kuniaki (May); the Re-Establishing Business Enterprises Ordinance is implemented (June); the second movement to enhance wartime mining production is implemented, sponsored by the Kokumin Soryoku Chosen Kozan Renmei (September); movements to promote the expansion of production capacity are implemented throughout Korea (November); the Korea Farmland Development Corporation is established (December).		
1943	Customs clearance procedures between Korea and Manchuria are simplified; the first meeting of the Agricultural Projections Committee is held (January); the Tasado Railway Line between Sinuiju and Namsi is nationalized; the Ordinance of Electric Power management in Korea is implemented; the Korea Oil Monopoly Ordinance is promulgated; a munitions production responsibility system is implemented (April); the Association for Control over the Distribution of Coke in Korea is established (May); opening ceremony is held for the Korea Weapons Industry Association; the Ordinance for Control over the Distribution of Coal in	Japanese Rule (Koiso Kuniaki)	

Year	Event	Administrator (The Governor-General)
	Korea is promulgated (June); the Korea Foodstuffs Management Ordinance is promulgated; the Ordinance Concerning Increased Production of Important Minerals is extended by five years (August); guidelines for increasing production and strengthening the workforce are published; the Korea Foodstuffs Corporation is established (October); the Korea Key Commodities Corporation is established (December).	
1944	A roundtable discussion on land management is sponsored by the Agricultural and Commerce Bureau, focusing on strengthening the mobilization of absentee landlords (January); guidelines are finalized for the implementation of an agricultural production responsibility system; the National Requisition Ordinance is invoked; an increase in indirect taxes is implemented (February); policies are finalized concerning the development of rare-element minerals; guidelines for promoting landowner activity, for implementing land management, and concerning underperforming farmers are published; additional compensation to be paid to Korean bureaucrats working in Korea is announced (March); four railway lines are nationalized, including the Hwanghae Line belonging to Chosen Tetsudo Kabushiki Kaisha; a military draft system is introduced (initiation of draft inspections); guidelines concerning the period of increased light metals production in the decisive stage of the war are published; school meals for pupils in major cities are initiated (April); the National Vocational Ability Declaration Ordinance is implemented (May); Governor-General Koiso steps down and is replaced by Army General Abe Nobuyuki (July); the Women's Volunteer Labor Ordinance is implemented (October); the full length of the Baengmu Line is opened; the Munitions Companies Act is implemented (December).	Japanese Rule (Koiso Kuniaki)
1945	The National Labor Mobilization Ordinance is implemented (April); the Research Center on Continental Resources, attached to Keijo Imperial University, is opened (June); the Korea General Headquarters of the Volunteer Corps is established; the Kokumin Soryoku Chosen Renmei is disbanded (July); the Soviet Union declares war on Japan and invades Manchuria, northern Korea, and southern Sakhalin (August 8–9); the Japanese government notifies the Allies of its acceptance of the Potsdam Declaration (August 14); Soviet troops occupy Pyongyang (about August 20); American General Douglas MacArthur announces his intention to divide Korea into two territories occupied respectively by the United States and the Soviet Union, with the boundary set at the 38th parallel; the United States Army Military Government in Korea is established in southern Korea (September).	Japanese Rule (Abe Nobuyuki)
1946	The Provisional People's Committee of North Korea is established (chaired by Kim Il-sung) (February); northern Korea implements land reform (March); northern Korea nationalizes important industries; the	American and Soviet military rule

Year	Event	Administrator (The Governor-General)		
	Workers' Party of North Korea is founded (August); the Workers' Party of South Korea is founded (November); the South Korea Transitional Legislative Assembly opens (December).			
1947	The People's Committee of North Korea is established (February); northern Korea implements currency reform (December).			
1948	The Korean People's Army is established (February); the Republic of Korea is founded with Syngman Rhee as president (August); the Republic of Korea Armed Forces is established; the Democratic People's Republic of Korea is founded, with Kim Il-sung as premier (September); Soviet forces withdraw from North Korea (December).			
1949	The Land Reform Act is promulgated in South Korea; American troops withdraw from South Korea; the Workers' Party of Korea is founded (the Workers' Party of North Korea absorbs the Workers' Party of South Korea) (June).			
1950	The Korean People's Army crosses the 38th parallel and invades the south (June 25).			
1953	The Korean Armistice Agreement is signed (July).			
1954	North Korea decides to pursue the thorough collectivization of agriculture (November).			
1958	North Korea completes the collectivization of agriculture (August).			
1960	The April Revolution occurs in South Korea and President Syngman Rhee steps down (April).	Republic of Korea	Democratic People's Republic of Korea	
1961	Army Major General Park Chung-hee seizes power in a coup d'état in South Korea (May).			
1968	North Korean special forces attack the executive office and official residence of the South Korean President (the Blue House) (January).			
1974	An attempt is made to assassinate President Park Chung-hee (the first lady is killed) (August).			
1979	President Park Chung-hee is assassinated (October).			
1980	Kim Jong-il is selected as a member of the Central Committee of the Workers' Party of Korea (October).			
1983	North Korean agents stage a terrorist bombing in Rangoon in an attempt to assassinate South Korean President Chun Doo-hwan (October).			
1987	South Korean presidential candidate Roh Tae-woo makes his "democratization declaration" (June); North Korean agents blow up a Korean Air passenger jet (November).			
1991	Kim Jong-il is appointed Supreme Commander of the Korean People's			

Year	Event	Administrator (The Governor-General)
	Army (December).	
1994	Kim Il-sung dies (July).	
2006	North Korea announces its first successful underground nuclear test (October).	
2011	Kim Jong-il dies (December).	

Selected Bibliography

A partial list of major works cited and other important sources. For a complete list of references, see works marked with an asterisk.

Books and Articles in Japanese and Korean

Bank of Japan. 1966. *Meiji iko hompo shuyo keizai tokei* [Hundred-Year Statistics of the Japanese Economy]. Tokyo: Bank of Japan.

Chosen Ginko Chosabu [The Bank of Chosen Research Division]. 1948. *Chosen keizai nempo 1948* [Annual Economic Report of Korea 1948]. Seoul: The Bank of Chosen. (In Korean)

Chosen Nokai. 1944a. *Chosen nogyo hattatsu shi: Hattatsu hen.* [The History of the Development of Korean Agriculture: Development]. Seoul: Chosen Nokai.

———. 1944b. *Chosen nogyo hattatsu shi: Seisaku hen* [The History of the Development of Korean Agriculture: Policies]. Seoul: Chosen Nokai.

Ch'oe Chongo. 2013. "Souru Daigakko ni okeru Keijo Teidai hogaku no isan: Hobungakubu hogakka o chushin ni" [Keijo Imperial University's Heritage of Law at Seoul National University: With a Focus on the Law and Literature Departments]. In *Empire and Higher Education in East Asia*, edited by Sakai Tetsuya and Matsuda Toshihiko, International Research Center for Japanese Studies International Symposium (Proceedings) 42: 213–228.

Committee for Editing the History of Korea Tungsten Co., ed. 1989. *A 70-Year History of Korea Tungsten Co.* Daegu: Korea Tungsten Co., Ltd. (In Korean)

Communist Party of Korea, North Korea Branch, Propaganda Department. 1946. *Understanding Land Reform in North Korea (draft).* Pyongyang: Communist Party of Korea, North Korea Branch, Publicity Department. (In Korean)

Eckert, Carter J. 2004. *Nihon teikoku no moshigo: Kochan no Kimu ichizoku to Kankoku shihonshugi no shokuminchi kigen 1876–1945.* Translated by Kotani Masayo. Tokyo: Soshisha. Originally published in 1991 as *Offspring of Empire: The Koch'ang Kims and the Colonial Origins of Korean Capitalism, 1876–1945.* Seattle and London: University of Washington Press.

The Government-General of Korea. 1922. *Chosen Sotokufu shisei nempo Taisho 10 nendo* [Annual Administration Report of the Government-General of Korea 1921]. Seoul: The Government-General of Korea.

———. 1911–1944. *Chosen Sotokufu tokei nempo: Dai 4-ji-Showa 17 nen* [Statistical Yearbook of the Government-General of Korea]. Seoul: The Government-General of Korea.

——. 1944. *Nogyo tokei hyo Showa 15 nen* [Table of Agricultural Statistics 1940]. Seoul: The Government-General of Korea.

——, ed. 1999. *Zoho Chosen Sotokufu 30-nen shi (1)–(3)* [Revised Edition: A 30-Year History of the Government-General of Korea (1)–(3)]. Tokyo: Kress Publishing.

Hagiwara Hikozo. 2001a. *Chosen Sotokufu kansei to sono gyosei kiko* [The Government-General of Korea's Regulations and Administrative Organs]. In *Chosen kindai shiryo kenkyu: Yuho shirizu* [Historical Sources on Modern Korean: Yuho Series], vol. 6, edited by Yuho Kyokai. Tokyo: Kress Publishing.

——. 2001b. *Nihon tochika no Chosen ni okeru Chosengo kyoiku* [Korean Language Education in Korea under Japanese Rule]. In *Chosen kindai shiryo kenkyu: Yuho shirizu* [Historical Sources on Modern Korean: Yuho Series], vol. 6, edited by Yuho Kyokai. Tokyo: Kress Publishing.

Hamauzu Tetsuo. 1991. *Eikoku shinshi no shokuminchi tochi: Indo koto bunkan e no michi* [British Gentlemen's Colonial Rule: The Road to High Posts in the Indian Civil Service]. Tokyo: Chuokoron-Shinsha, Inc.

Han Yeong-u. 2016. *Our modern history opening the future.* Seoul: Gyeongse-won. (In Korean)

Harada Keikichi. 1946. "Funada Kyoji *'Roma Ho'* Zen 5-kan" [*Roman Law* by Funada Kyoji, All 5 Volumes]. *Kokka Gakkai Zasshi* [The Journal of the Association of Political and Social Sciences] 60 (4): 33–46.

Hirai Koichi. 1997. *Nihon shokuminchi zaiseishi kenkyu* [Study of Public Finance in the Japanese Colonies]. Kyoto: Minerva Shobo.

Huh Nam Jung. 2016. *Konmei suru Nikkan kankei o dakai seyo! Imakoso Paku Tejun ni manabo. Paku Tejun ga kotaeda.* [Overcome the Confusion in the Japan-Korea Relationship! Learn from Park Taejoon. He is the Answer!]. Translated by Tsutsumi Kazunao. Machida: Institute for Northeast Asian Studies, J. F. Oberlin University.

Iinuma Jiro. 1982. "Nitteika Chosen ni okeru nogyo kakumei" [The Agricultural Revolution in Korea under Japanese Imperialism]. In *Shokuminchi-ki Chosen no shakai to teiko* [Society and Resistance in Colonial Korea], edited by Iinuma Jiro and Kang Jae-eon. Tokyo: Miraisha.

Iwasaki Ikuo and Hagiwara Yoshiyuki, eds. 1996. *ASEAN shokoku no kanryoseiji* [The Bureaucracy in ASEAN countries]. Tokyo: Institute of Developing Economies.

Ju Ik-jong. 2005. "Standards of Living in Colonial Korea—Reexamining the Debate." In *New History of Korean Economic Development: From the Late Joseon Dynasty to Rapid Economic Growth in the Twentieth Century*, edited by Yi Dae-geun et al. Seoul: Nanam Publishing House. (In Korean)

Kang Jae-eon, ed. 1985. *Kitachosen ni okeru Nicchitsu Kontserun* [The Nicchitsu

Industrial Complex in North Korea]. Tokyo: Fuji Shuppan.

Kawai Kazuo. 1986. *Chosen ni okeru sanmai zoshoku keikaku* [Rice Production Development Program in Korea]. Tokyo: Miraisha.

Kim Nak-nyeon, ed. 2008. *Shokuminchi-ki Chosen no kokumin keizai keisan 1910–1945* [Economic Growth in Korea 1910–1945]. Translated by Moon Ho-il and Kim Seung-mi. Tokyo: University of Tokyo Press.

Kim Yeong-hui. 2014. *Bosei ni yoru ningen no taika: Hokkan shakai no shintai waisho ni kansuru kenkyu.* [Human Atrophy by Tyranny: Research on Dwarfism in North Korea]. Translated by Hong Hyeong. Tokyo: Publishing Department of One Korea Daily News.

Kimura Mitsuhiko. 1983. "Shokuminchika Chosen no mensaku ni tsuite" [On the Production of Cotton in Colonial Korea]. *Aziya Kenkyu* 30 (1): 54–79.

*———. 1991. "Shokuminchiki Chosen ni okeru seikatsu suijun no henka: Shincho deta o megutte" [Changes in the Standards of Living in Colonial Korea: On Data Concerning People's Heights]. *Osaka Daigaku Keizaigaku* [Osaka Economic Papers] 41 (2 and 3): 206–217.

*———. 1999a. *Kitachosen no keizai: Kigen, keisei, hokai* [The Economy of North Korea: Origin, Formation, and Collapse]. Tokyo: Sobunsha.

———. 2016. *Kitachosen keizaishi 1910–1960* [Economic History of North Korea 1910–1960]. Tokyo: Chisen Shokan.

*Kimura Mitsuhiko and Abe Keiji. 2003. *Kitachosen no gunji kogyoka: Teikoku no senso kara Kin Nissei no senso e* [Military Industrialization in North Korea: From the Empire's War to Kim Il-sung's War]. Tokyo: Chisen Shokan.

Kishi Hidetsugu. 1914. "Chosen shono kyusai no ichi-hosaku" [A Measure for Saving Korean Peasants]. *Chosen Nokaiho* 9 (9): 12–17.

Lee Young-hoon. 2009. *Daikan Minkoku no monogatari* [The Story of the Republic of Korea]. Translated by Nagashima Hiroki. Tokyo: Bungeishunju.

Lim Chaisung. 2005. *Senji keizai to testudo un'ei: Shokuminchi keizai kara bundan Kankoku e no rekishiteki keiro o saguru* [Wartime Economy and Railway Policies: Searching the History of Korea from Colonial Korea to the Divided Peninsula]. Tokyo: University of Tokyo Press.

Ministry of Finance, ed. 1958. *Meiji Taisho zaiseishi dai 18-kan gaichi zaisei jo* [History of Public Finance of the Meiji and Taisho Periods, vol. 18, Public Finance in the Overseas Territories, vol. 1]. Tokyo: Keizai Orai-sha.

Miyazaki Masayoshi. 1938. *Toa renmei ron* [On the East Asian League]. Tokyo: Kaizosha.

Mizuta Naomasa ed. 1974a. *Sotokufu jidai no zaisei: Chosen kindai zaisei no kakuritsu* [Public Finance under the Government-General of Korea: The

Establishment of Modern Korean Public Finance]. Tokyo: Yuho Kyokai.

———. 1974b. *Tokanfu jidai no zaisei: Chosen kindai zaisei no jigatame* [Public Finance under the Residency-General of Korea: Laying the Foundations of Modern Korean Public Finance]. Tokyo: Yuho Kyokai.

Munakata Eiji. 2001. *Michi o hiraku watashi no gijutsu kaihatsushi* [Path to the Future: My History of Technology Development]. Tokyo: Nikkan Shobo.

Norinsho Nettai Nogyo Kenkyu Senta, ed. 1976. *Kyu Chosen ni okeru Nihon no nogyo shiken kenkyu no seika* [The Results of Japanese Agricultural Research Tests in Korea]. Tokyo: Norin Tokei Kyokai.

Nosei Chosakai, ed. 1977. *Kaitei Nihon nogyo kiso tokei* [Basic Agricultural Statistics of Japan, revised]. Tokyo: Norin Tokei Kyokai.

Ohkawa Kazushi, Takamatsu Nobukiyo, and Yamamoto Yuzo. 1987. *Choki keizai tokei 1 kokumin shotoku* [Long-Term Economic Statistics 1, National Income]. Tokyo: Toyo Keizai Shimposha.

Okamoto Makiko. 2008. *Shokuminchi kanryo no seijishi: Chosen, Taiwan Sotokufu to teikoku Nippon* [History of Colonial Bureaucracy: The Government-Generals of Korea and Taiwan, and Imperial Japan]. Tokyo: Sangensha.

Park Kyung-sik. 1993. *Nihon teikoku shugi no Chosen shihai* [Ruling Korea under Japanese Imperialism], vols. 1 and 2. Tokyo: Aoki Shoten.

The Residency-General of Korea. 1907–1910. *Tokanfu tokei nempo dai-ichiji-dai-sanji* [Statistical Yearbook of the Residency-General of Korea, vols. 1–3]. Seoul: The Residency-General of Korea.

Sato Atsushi. 1970. "Funada Kyoji cho 'Roma Ho' dai 1-kan (koho, hogen), dai 2-kan (shiho dai-ichi bunsatsu soron, bukken)" [*Roman Law* by Funada Kyoji, volume 1 (Public Law and Source of Law), volume 2 (Separate Volume of Private Law and Real Rights)]. *Hoseishi Kenkyu* [Legal History Research] 1970 (20): 238–239.

Shibuya Reiji, ed. 1939. *Chosen gijutsusha meibo* [List of Engineers in Korea]. Chosen Kogyo Kyokai. Reprinted in Haga Noboru et al., eds. 2001. *Nihon jinbutsu joho taikei* [Biographies of Japanese], vol. 78, Korean Section 8. Tokyo: Koseisha.

Shimotomai Nobuo. 2004. *Ajia reisenshi* [History of the Cold War in Asia]. Tokyo: Chuokoron-Shinsha.

Shinohara Miyohei. 1981. *Choki keizai tokei 10 kokogyo* [Long-Term Economic Statistics 10, Mining and Manufacturing]. Tokyo: Toyo Keizai Shimposha.

Showajuku Jukuyukai, ed. 1991. *Kaiso no Showajuku* [Showajuku in Recollection]. Kawasaki: Showajuku Jukuyukai.

Tohata Seiichi and Ohkawa Kazushi. 1935. *Chosen beikoku keizai ron* [The Rice Economy in Korea]. Tokyo: Nihon Gakujitsu Shinko Kai.

———. 1939. *Chosen beikoku keizai ron* [The Rice Economy in Korea]. In *Beikoku keizai no kenkyu* [Research on Rice Economies], edited by Kawata Shiro. Tokyo: Yuhikaku Publishing.

Umemura Mataji and Mizoguchi Toshiyuki, eds. 1988. *Kyu Nihon shokuminchi keizai tokei suikei to bunseki* [Economic Statistics of the Former Japanese Colonies: Estimates and Analysis]. Tokyo: Toyo Keizai Shimposha.

Watanabe Toshio. 1978. *Kaihatsu keizaigaku kenkyu* [Research into Developming Economics]. Tokyo: Toyo Keizai Shimposha.

Wickizer, V.D. and M.K. Bennett. 1958. *Monsuun Ajia no beikoku keizai*, translated by Tamai Torao and Hirota Yoshio. Tokyo: Nihon Hyoron Shinsha. Originally published in 1941 as *The Rice Economy of Monsoon Asia*. Stanford: Stanford University Press.

Yamabe Kentaro. 1971. *Nihon tochika no Chosen* [Korea under Japanese Rule]. Tokyo: Iwanami Shoten.

Yamamoto Yuzo. 1992. *Nihon shokuminchi keizaishi kenkyu* [Research into the Economic History of Japan's Colonies]. Nagoya: The University of Nagoya Press.

Yi Dae-geun. 2015. *Study of Reverted Property: Colonial Heritage and the Course of the Korean Economy.* Seoul: Isup. (In Korean)

Yi Hyeong-nang. 2015. *Shokuminchi Chosen no kome to Nihon: Beikoku kensa seido no tenkai katei* [Rice in Colonial Korea and Japan: The Development Process of the Rice-Inspection System]. Tokyo: Chuo University Press.

Yoshida Keiichi. 1954. *Chosen suisan kaihatsu shi* [The History of the Development of the Korean Marine Products Industry]. Shimonoseki: Chosuikai.

Yukizawa Kenzo and Maeda Shozo. 1978. *Nihon boeki no choki tokei: Boeki kozoshi kenkyu no kiso sagyo* [Long-Term Statistics on Japanese Foreign Trade: Basic Steps for Research on the History of Trade Structures]. Tokyo: Dohosha.

Zenkoku Keizai Chosa Rengokai Chosen Shibu, ed. 1943. *Chosen keizai nempo Showa 16, 17 nen* [Annual Economic Report of Korea 1941, 1942]. Tokyo: Kaizosha.

Books and Articles in English

Kim Duol and Heejin Park. 2011. "Measuring Living Standards from the Lowest: Height of the Male *Hangryu* Deceased in Colonial Korea," *Explorations in Economic History* 48: 590–599.

*Kimura Mitsuhiko. 1986. "A Note on Periodic Markets in Korea, 1914-1940: An Economist's Viewpoint," *Canadian Geographer* 30 (4): 343–350.

———. 1989. "Public Finance in Korea under Japanese Rule: Deficit in the Colonial Account and Colonial Taxation," *Explorations in Economic History* 26: 285–310.

———. 1993. "Standards of Living in Colonial Korea: Did the Masses Become Worse

Off or Better Off under Japanese Rule?" *Journal of Economic History* 53 (3): 629–652.

*———. 1995. "The Economics of Japanese Imperialism in Korea, 1910-1939," *Economic History Review* XLVIII (3): 555–574.

*———. 1999b. "From Fascism to Communism: Continuity and Development of Collectivist Economic Policy in North Korea," *Economic History Review* LII (1): 69–86.

———. forthcoming. "Ethnic income distribution in colonial Korea and Taiwan," *Aoyama Kokusai Seikei Ronshu* [The Aoyama Journal of International Politics, Economics and Communication].

Myint, Hla. 1965. *The Economics of the Developing Countries.* New York: Praeger.

———. 1971. *Economic Theory and the Underdeveloped Countries.* New York: Oxford University Press.

Ohkawa Kazushi and Shinohara Miyohei, eds. 1979. *Patterns of Japanese Economic Development: A Comparative Appraisal.* New Haven: Yale University Press.

Zhebin, Alexander. 2000. "A Political History of Soviet-North Korean Nuclear Cooperation." In *The North Korean Nuclear Program: Security, Strategy, and New Perspectives from Russia,* edited by James Clay Moltz and Alexandre Y. Mansourov, 27–40. New York and London: Routledge.

Journals

Chosen Nokaiho [Report of the Agricultural Association of Korea].

Koan Chosa Geppo [Monthly Investigative Report on Public Security].

Index

Note: Page number in italics refers to illustrations. The abbreviation 't' refers to tables.

rice-husking/-polishing plants 25,
71–73, 95, 130, 170, 196t
RIKEN *see* Institute of Physical and
Chemical Research
road networks 40, 41, 80, 103, 141, 198
rocket fuel manufacture 147, 158–59,
160, 161, 170
Rogo-otsuyaku rocket fuel 159
Roma ho (Roman Law) (Funada) 191,
192
Roman Law Library (Keijo Imperial
University) 191–92
rubber processing plants 86, 89, 164t
Rural and Mountain Village Production
and Patriotism Campaign (Nosanson
Seisan Hokoku Undo) 123, 211t
Rural Revitalization Campaign (Noson
Shinko Undo) 123
Russo-Japanese War (1904-1905) 15,
204t
Ryuto Kogyosho 74
Ryuzan Kosaku 89, 131
Ryuzan Kosaku Kabushiki Kaisha
(Ryuzan Manufacturing Company) 89

S

Saemaeul Undong (New Village
Movement) 183
Saito Makoto (Admiral) 37, 207t, 208t,
209t
Sakushin Gakuin 191
Samcheok coal mine 74, 139
Sanchoku Kaihatsu (Sanchoku
Development) 74
Sanmai Zoshoku Keikaku (Rice
Production Development Program)
64–65, 66, 122, 123, 195, 207t, 201t
Sansei Kogyo 142

Sansei Kogyo Yongampo Smelting
Works 154
Sariwon coal mine 75–76, 139
Second Japan-Korea Convention (1905)
15, 205t
Sengoku period 19
seodang schools 27–28, 29
Seongjin Plant 78, 148, 149, 165t, 166t
sericulture 25–26, 68–70, 74, 80, 81,
212t
Shinagawa Shirorenga 142, 167t
Shin Ung-ho 112, 113t
Showa Academy 172
Showa Denko 144, 156t, 157t, 165t
Showa Seikosho (Showa Ironworks)
150, 158
Shunsen Nogyo Gakko 172
Siemens 75
silica sand industries 136t, 144
silk industry 25–26, 68–70, 74, 80–81,
97, 212t
silver mining 18, 19, 78, 91t, 153, 154,
177
socialism 173, 185, 189, 202
sock-knitting industry 82
soft (smoky) coal 74–76, 139–40
South Manchuria Railway Company 36,
50, 51, 56, 81, 206t, 208t, 210t
Soviet Union 87, 97, 139, 189, 213t,
214t
North Korea 176, 180, 181, 182,
184–85, 186–87, 188
soybeans 21, 22, 67–68, 70, 85, 206t,
211t
Special Account for Extraordinary
Military Spending 121, 122
Special Fighting Spirit Corps 132
spiritual mobilization programs 123,
124, 211t

About the Author

Kimura Mitsuhiko

Born in Tokyo, he studied at Hokkaido University and Osaka University in Japan, and London School of Economics and Political Science (LSE) in the UK. He was a professor in the School of International Politics, Economics, and Communication at Aoyama Gakuin University in Tokyo from 1999 to 2020. Currently, he is professor emeritus at the same university. He specializes in East Asian Economics.

（英文版）日本統治下の朝鮮　統計と実証研究は何を語るか
The Economics of Colonialism in Korea: Rethinking Japanese Rule and Aftermath

2021年3月27日　第1刷発行
2021年4月27日　第2刷発行

著　者　木村光彦
英　訳　公益財団法人日本国際問題研究所
発行所　一般財団法人出版文化産業振興財団
　　　　〒101-0051 東京都千代田区神田神保町2-2-30
　　　　電話　03-5211-7283
　　　　ホームページ　https://www.jpic.or.jp/

印刷・製本所　大日本印刷株式会社

© 2018 Kimura Mitsuhiko
Printed in Japan
ISBN 978-4-86658-124-8